"Then Roy Said to Mickey..."

"Then **Roy** Said to **Mickey...**"

The Best Yankees Stories Ever Told

Roy White with Darrell Berger

TRIUMPH
BOOKS

Library of Congress Cataloging-in-Publication Data

White, Roy, 1943–
   Then Roy said to Mickey : the best Yankees stories ever told by Roy White with Darrell Berger.
      p. cm.
   Includes bibliographical references.
   ISBN 978-1-60078-091-2
   1. New York Yankees (Baseball team)—Anecdotes. 2. Baseball—New York (State)—New York—History—20th century—Anecdotes. 3. White, Roy, 1943– —Anecdotes. 4. Mantle, Mickey, 1931–1995—Anecdotes. I. Berger, Darrell, 1948– II. Title.
   GV875.N4W55 2009
   796.357'64097471—dc22
                                              2008048342

This book is available in quantity at special discounts for your group or organization. For further information, contact:

Triumph Books
542 South Dearborn Street
Suite 750
Chicago, Illinois 60605
(312) 939-3330
Fax (312) 663-3557

Printed in U.S.A.
ISBN: 978-1-60078-091-2
Design by Patricia Frey
Photos courtesy of AP Images except where otherwise indicated

To all of my former coaches and managers who helped to make me a Major League Baseball player:

Dave Carlye (high school)
Mr. Silas (American Legion)
Mr. Butts (Connie Mack)
Loren Babe
Rube Walker
Wally Moses
Johnny Keane
Ralph Houk

—Roy White

To my mother, La Donna Berger, who never threw away my baseball cards.

—Darrell Berger

table of contents

acknowledgments

Our deep thanks and appreciation to everyone who shared their stories and memories with us, including Marty Appel, Rich Beck, Paul Blair, Ron Blomberg, Jim Bouton, Chris Chambliss, Ian Dixon, Al Downing, Whitey Ford, Oscar Gamble, Jake Gibbs, Ernie Harwell, Henry Hecht, Jim Kaat, Arturo Lopez, Billy Martin Jr., Sam McDowell, Gene Monahan, Bobby Murcer, Phil Pepe, Joe Pepitone, Fritz Peterson, Mike Siler, and Dooley Womack.

Roy would also like to thank his family, the New York Yankees organization, and the greatest baseball fans in America—New York Yankees fans.

Darrell thanks the Larry Ritter and Mike Gershman Memorial Monthly Lunch Bunch, going strong since 1991, including Billy Altman, Marty Appel, Ev Begley, Bob Costas, Bob Creamer, David Falkner, Stan Isaacs, Lee Lowenfish, Ernestine Miller, Ray Robinson, Brian Silverman, Al Silverman, and Willie Weinbaum. Also, thanks to Frank and Vivian Barning, who first encouraged Darrell as a baseball writer in *Baseball Hobby News*. Darrell says, "Special thanks also to my wife, Kathleen. The day I married her was my own personal walk-off homer."

Both Roy and Darrell thank John Monteleone, agent and literary mentor, who encouraged and improved our efforts from first pitch to final out.

introduction

Roy White is the only Yankee who played as a regular with both Mickey Mantle and Mickey Rivers. His career is the only link between one great Yankees era and the next. He came up as a rookie in 1965, not yet old enough to vote. He played with Mantle, Ford, Boyer, Richardson, Maris, and Pepitone at the end of their glory years. Then, as the senior Yankee in point of service among free agents and trade acquisitions, he played with Jackson, Nettles, Chambliss, Munson, Dent, and Piniella and won three pennants and two world championships from 1976 through 1978.

This book is written in Roy's voice and from his point of view, but it is not a Roy White autobiography, though I hope he gets around to writing it one day. Although some of the stories have Roy as the central figure, more of them are about his teammates. Among stars who shone brightly, talked loudly, and behaved as though the spotlights and microphones were always near, Roy was a quiet guy. He was, and still is, a classy guy.

Some of these stories cover decades, even whole careers. Others recount one day, one pitch, or one swing. The reader need not proceed from front cover to back. Jump around. Read for two minutes or 60.

The first chapter features three superstars—Catfish Hunter, new Hall of Famer Goose Gossage, and Thurman Munson. The public perception of them is sometimes accurate, sometimes completely mistaken. These stories show how their teammates knew them.

Roy White's isn't the only career that bridges one era of Yankees greatness with another. The second chapter shows how Whitey Ford and Mel Stottlemyre connected to form two links in the chain of pitching wisdom passed down through a lineage of smart hurlers who knew how to throw a curve for a strike on 2–0. Ancient Satchel Paige is also here, giving an adolescent Al Downing the pitcher's equivalent of "Use the force, Luke."

When Roy signed a Yankees contract in 1961, he thought he was joining a juggernaut. When he arrived in the Bronx four years later, the wheels had fallen off. Although some new Yankees such as Roy and Bobby Murcer completed distinguished careers, more often they were thwarted by injuries. Ron Blomberg, Jake Gibbs, and Dooley Womack tell their stories of great promise unfulfilled. Ian Dixon and Rich Beck had arms as good as most in the majors, but far worse luck.

Roy established himself as a solid regular in the 1970s. At this time, the Yankees were wallowing in mediocrity and injuries, but that was not the whole story. Their new owner, CBS, knew how to run a profitable television network but not a winning baseball team.

Roy did allow us to include a little about his early life, squeezed into the middle of everything here. He grew up in Compton, California, back when it bragged that more active major leaguers had grown up there than any other town in America. As an African American, Roy's early minor-league and spring-training experiences in the South in the early 1960s show that he had more to overcome than curveballs and sliding bruises.

After 11 years in the majors, Roy was finally able to play on some historically great teams. In what has been called "the Bronx Zoo," Roy was a camel. He didn't make much noise, didn't need or get much attention, but carried a lot of weight in the clubhouse and on the field. Although he did not make many of the historic Yankees hits of the era, he was on base for an astonishing number of them. This was no accident.

He did what he was asked to do. From year to year he didn't know where he would hit in the order. If a cleanup hitter was needed, Roy hit fourth. If a leadoff was needed, Roy did that. After being shuffled around the infield and outfield as a youngster, he settled in left, where he played its Yankee Stadium vastness sometimes literally to perfection.

One year he didn't make an error. Other years he didn't miss a game. He was the epitome of the guy who does the little things to win. Hit and run. Hit behind the runner. Steal a base when it matters. Hit the ball into the outfield to get the runner in from third. Play through injuries. If you can't throw out the runner at home, hit the cutoff man. If a fan picked Roy as his favorite Yankee, it marked that fan as an insider of sophisticated taste, like someone who prefers single-malt Scotch to the blended stuff.

The men who speak here represent the spectrum of professional baseball players. Some had their hopes for a long major league career dashed. Others played enough to get on some baseball cards and be celebrities in their hometowns. A few are known to every baseball fan and beyond. The things they all have in common is that they all like and respect Roy White, and they all loved being Yankees.

—Darrell Berger

chapter 1

Three of the Best

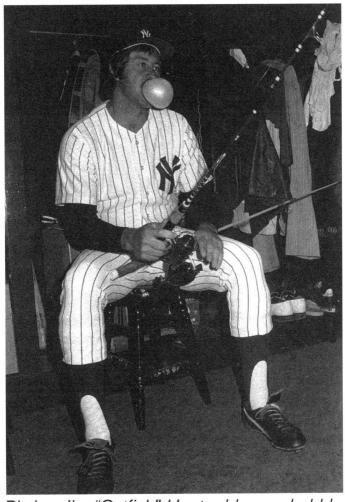

Pitcher Jim "Catfish" Hunter blows a bubble in the locker room at Shea Stadium prior to making his Yankees pitching debut against the Detroit Tigers on April 11, 1975.

Catfish for Always

Roy Campanella once said that in order to play baseball you have to be a man, but you have to have a lot of little boy in you, too. Most major leaguers fall somewhere in between, at least when they start. I signed my first professional contract several years before I could vote.

That midpoint between boyhood and manhood tends to be extended in baseball players, which has its good and bad points. A major leaguer has to retain the enthusiasm and joy for the game he had as a kid, or else he will never tolerate or cope with the frustrations and pressures of playing the game at its highest levels.

But the game can also give a player a case of terminal adolescence. That's why so many of us have a hard time adjusting to life after baseball. It's not just a matter of no longer getting a big paycheck. It's time to grow up, and some of us aren't ready.

I think Jim "Catfish" Hunter was born an adult. I don't know of any other player, or any man I've ever met, who lived life on such an even keel. He was very composed and easy to talk to. When he got the biggest contract in baseball to come to the Yankees in 1975, you would have never known it to talk to him. To see him walk into Yankee Stadium, you couldn't tell if he was there to pitch or paint the concession stands. He was the same guy all the time. In the clubhouse after a game, you wouldn't know if he pitched a shutout or gave up nine runs in the first. There were no highs and lows. Remember when teachers took attendance in school, sometimes you answered, "present"? That was Hunter. He was present.

Regardless of what straw stirred whose drink, the player that got us to championship level was Jim Hunter. Charlie Finley, the A's owner when Hunter was a rookie, gave him the nickname Catfish to add a little color to a guy who was so regular he was extraordinary. Finley knew his geography pretty well. Hunter came from Hertford, North Carolina, a bustling metropolis of about 2,000 people, in the northeast section of the state known as "the Inner Banks." Fishing is huge there, and I'm guessing Jim might have reeled in a few cats as a kid.

Jim was born, raised, died, and is buried in Hertford, having sadly succumbed to Lou Gehrig's Disease in 1999 at age 53. That's why he's not better-known today, even though he is a Hall of Famer. To give you an idea of how much Hunter was part of Hertford, even when he was pitching before thousands in the Bronx, there was a street named after him back in Hertford. It is Jimmy Hunter Drive. Not Catfish Hunter, not Jim "Catfish" Hunter Drive. Jimmy. You get the idea that they would have named a street after him if he'd been a plumber. He would have been the most stand-up, regular, dependable plumber anyone had ever seen.

He won at least 20 games five years in a row, four times for the A's and once with us, and would have won more if the A's had gotten good a little sooner. He pitched 30 complete games in 1975, the last pitcher to have that many. *Really* the last one. Roy Halladay led the majors in 2008 with nine. Another 30-complete-game season is far less likely than another 30-win season. The last pitcher to have more than 30 was Robin Roberts, who had 33 back in 1953.

Jim was one baseball cliché come true. He threw like he was sitting in a rocking chair. His nice, easy motion would smoothly lead to a comfortable 0–4. I ought to know. I hit a big, fat .206 against him, so I was glad to see him put on the pinstripes for several reasons.

His complete games didn't necessarily rack up high pitch counts. He pitched with economy. He didn't go 2–2, 3–2 on every batter, like so many pitchers today. He wasn't watching a radar-gun posting on the scoreboard to see how often he hit 90 or 95. He wasn't trying to miss bats; he was succeeding in hitting them just a little bit, yielding dinky grounders and pop-flies.

When he pitched those 30 complete games, he pitched only 10 more innings than the year before, but, as baseball experts know today, the stress on the arm isn't just because of a lot of innings, it's what *kind* of innings. He pitched 23 complete games the previous year, so those 30 meant even more eighth innings, more ninth innings, and once, a tenth. In his 39 starts, he failed to pitch seven full innings only twice.

His arm was never the same. The following year he pitched almost as much, but his earned-run average was nearly a full run higher, and he failed to win 20, settling for 17–15, even though we were a better team. The year after that he pitched about half as much and had become a sore-armed pitcher, winning nine and losing nine.

There is a familiar theme in the stories about pitchers. At some point they all say, "Then I hurt my arm." Or worse, "Then my arm just went dead." Maybe it is Whitey Ford after a Hall of Fame career. Maybe it is Jim Bouton after one great year. Maybe it is Al Downing, who lost his blazing fastball but learned how to pitch and had enough left to be a winner, even if his gigantic potential was never realized.

Catfish Hunter's arm was like the monster in the slasher movies. After you thought it was dead, it came back for one more big scene. He started 1978 just as he had finished 1977: bad. A big part of the reason the Red Sox got off to a huge lead was Hunter's injury. After a few poor starts, he couldn't wave good-bye. We thought we had waved goodbye to our meal ticket. It seemed like he had tried everything. Then an elderly doctor came into the clubhouse. From the procedure that followed, he was most likely an osteopath or a chiropractor.

Gene Monahan was there. Gene was the young trainer for the Yankees who rose to the position a couple years earlier from the Yankees' minor league system. He's still the Yankees trainer and so accomplished on the job that he was elected to the New York State Athletic Trainers' Association Hall of Fame in 2007. "This was not the first procedure of this type," Gene remembers, though it was rare and still is. "They put Catfish to sleep or heavily sedated him. Then they put his right arm into 90 degrees of abduction and 90 degrees of elbow flexion."

That, in layman's terms, translates to this: Imagine yourself flat on your back with your arm at your side. Raise your right hand so that it is sticking straight up, but keep your elbow on the table.

"The doctor forced external rotation," Gene continues, meaning that he moved the lower arm away from the body. "There was a loud pop." This description is similar to the standard procedure for adjusting a separated shoulder, though Hunter never received such a diagnosis. Whatever the problem, this treatment worked.

"He woke up with more external rotation, and this enabled him to cock his shoulder and arm more efficiently in the position where he could elicit more force rather naturally in his motion. It certainly did help," Monahan says. "Catfish actually threw that evening at the stadium afterward and was impressed, happy, and excited." For Hunter to appear excited, it must have been a major improvement, indeed.

In 11 starts in August and September, Hunter went 9–1 with five complete games. Without Hunter, Bucky Dent's fly never would have gone over the Green Monster, because we would have been home watching the postseason on television. Catfish won the sixth and final game of the World Series.

The effectiveness of the arm-pop did not last. The following year, it was like he never got loose. He became a once-a-week pitcher and started only 19 games scattered randomly throughout the year. It wasn't good, nothing helped, and Hunter went back to Hertford at age 33, having won 224 games. The monster that was Jimmy Hunter's arm was dead. By the same age, Roger Clemens had won only 182.

"Of all the players I have trained over more than 40 years, without mentioning or even hinting of a favorite, Catfish was one of a kind, who only comes around every 45 years or so. I mean that," Gene declares. "I've been asked a thousand times who was my favorite or what two or three were up there. I'll never name or decide on any one of my athletes. But I tell you...this one...would be right up there...for always."

Good for the Goose

Goose Gossage finally got into the Hall of Fame, and everybody who played with him agrees it was way overdue. It was great to get him on our side for the 1978 season, when he signed as a free agent. It was kind of strange, the way he was used as a kid on the White Sox.

He struggled during his first three years and started only eight games. We faced him in the stadium a few times and roughed him up pretty well. By the sixth inning, he'd be running out of gas, and we could start to catch up to his fastball. It was different when he was a reliever and had to go only one or two innings. It was a great feeling knowing the game was over when Goose came in. Nobody could touch him. I'm glad I never had to face him once he got settled as a reliever.

He had a great year of relief for Chicago in 1975, but the next year he was a starter almost exclusively. He didn't pitch that badly and completed 15 of 29 starts. But he pitched 224 innings, 82 more than the previous year, and recorded only five more strike-outs. He went back to the pen and didn't start another game in his entire career, which lasted 18 more years.

He is best remembered for his dominating years as a Yankees closer. People forget that he didn't exactly set the world on fire when he first came to New York. Or rather, he set *some* games on fire, which isn't what you want from your closer.

He was the big free agent, but he didn't automatically have the trust of his teammates. Some wondered why he was even with us, since we'd won the World Series the previous year, and Sparky Lyle, our closer, had won the Cy Young Award. Goose's first game was a big goose egg. Richie Zisk of the Rangers hit a walk-off homer in the bottom of the ninth in Arlington to win 2–1.

He next relieved Ken Holtzman with a 3–1 lead in the sixth inning in Milwaukee, with a runner on first and no outs. The first batter he faced was Larry Hisle. Hisle hit a home run to tie the game. The Brewers scored two in the following inning to win.

In his third game, he relieved Catfish Hunter in the fifth inning with two on and Baltimore ahead 3–1. The first batter was Doug DeCinces, who hit a two-run homer to make the score 5–1. Gossage didn't lose the game, but he didn't help.

His fourth game was more creative but yielded the same results. Goose pitched scoreless ball for three innings of a tie game, then let the winning run score when he made an error on an attempted sacrifice bunt.

It would have been funny if it wasn't so weird, because we knew Goose had the goods and wasn't one of those guys who "had trouble pitching in New York." Or so we still wanted to believe. It wasn't too long after these first few games that, with the other team starting to rally, the call came for Goose. At the time, we used a little car painted with pinstripes to bring relief pitchers into games. The car stopped in front the bullpen and waited for Gossage. Mickey Rivers was in center. He ran over to the car and tried to stop it. He laid down on the hood and rode on the car about halfway to the mound. We didn't know what to think, but the crowd thought it was pretty funny.

Goose finally came to the mound, and Thurman Munson walked out to meet him. Now, Munson was a guy who *never* thought anything was funny during a game. But as he was walking, he started to laugh. Why?

Munson pointed out to center field, where Rivers was hunkered down in a sprinter's stance, pointed out toward the fence. We more or less tried not to laugh. One player who certainly didn't think it was funny was Gossage. He got mad, got the hitters out, and he was great after that. Rivers knew what we needed to keep us loose. Goose knew what he needed to do to win over his teammates. Everybody did what was needed, and, against all odds, we came back and won the World Series again.

Goose had the reputation of being mean on the mound. He certainly looked mean, with his droopy gunfighter mustache. "He would turn his back on the batter at the plate," Oscar Gamble says. "That was a little upsetting if you were at bat. But Goose didn't try to hit batters. He didn't *care* if he hit batters, but he didn't try to. He had a lot of *good* streaks, but I remember in 1980 he had a stretch where he was almost unhittable."

That streak was from August 8 through September 21. He relieved in 18 games, pitching 27 innings. He allowed nine hits and six walks and struck out 36. No runs. None. Zero. More precisely, a goose egg.

Henry Hecht, who covered us for the *New York Post* during the entire length of Gossage's Yankees career, remembers, "Goose was a good ole boy from Colorado. He was liked by everybody." Henry also has a reason why Goose might have been so dominant during the stretch of 1980, without which the Yankees probably would not have passed the Orioles by three games to win the American League East.

As famous as his fastball was, Henry says, "He got a lot of outs on sliders. He could throw it for strikes, and hitters protecting themselves against the fastball couldn't adjust. When Rick Cerone came over in 1980, he pressed Gossage to use the slider even more." Not only did it help him in 1980, it extended his career, allowing him to be effective far longer than a reliever who depended exclusively on heat. It probably enabled him to amass Hall of Fame career numbers to go along with his peak years of dominance with us.

Even intimidators have their moments of doubt, however. When Goose turned his back on the batter, it wasn't always just to intimidate. Henry says, "Gossage admitted he was a little nervous with Yaz at bat in the ninth inning with two outs in the 1978 playoff game." He wasn't turning his back to make the batter sweat so much as to deal with his own emotions. "He said to himself, 'What's the worst thing that can happen? Tomorrow I'll be back home in Colorado.' He relaxed, threw a moving fastball, Yaz popped up." Yaz went home. Goose didn't see Colorado until after the parade.

Thurman as We Knew Him

Most players are basically the same on the field and off. Mickey Rivers was "Mick the Quick"—hard to pin down, hard to locate outside the ballpark, just as he was hard to throw out on the bases, a guy who would beat out a 12-hopper to second. Lou Piniella was intense, Willie Randolph composed, Sparky Lyle as devilish as his grin behind that huge mustache. I have a reputation

Thurman Munson limbers up his arm at spring-training camp in Ft. Lauderdale on February 24, 1978.

of being pretty quiet, efficient, and professional, if not exactly charismatic, and I'll own up to all that with an amount of pride that I hope falls somewhere between self-effacing and boastful.

The guy who was the most different from the guy the fans saw was Thurman Munson. The game face he presented was a scowl. He was terse and seldom helpful to sportswriters, so they wrote that he was at least uncooperative and maybe even a bad guy. In public, he looked like he was always mad, always grumpy.

"The writers never saw the true Munson," says Henry Hecht, the baseball beat writer for the *New York Post*. "He would only say, 'I'm just happy to be here.' After a while, you realized that was his more-or-less polite way of telling you to go to hell."

His locker was right next to mine. He was always the first guy I saw when I came to the park. We talked every day. He was one of my best friends on the team. I remember he always looked for me when we were on the road and he wanted a good place to eat. "When I want a gourmet dinner, I'm going out with Roy," Thurman would say. "I know he's not going to be eating the ham and cheese in the clubhouse." Like today's salaries, today's postgame meals in the clubhouse have been considerably upgraded. In my day, I just wanted to get away from the pizza and bologna as fast as I could.

The real Thurman Munson wasn't anything like the public grinch he pretended to be. That was all protective armor. He was a fun guy to be around. His teammates got to see his soft side, which contained a huge measure of love and attachment to his family back in Ohio. That's why he started flying, of course, so he could be with them more often during the season.

His family was the main reason for his returning to Ohio during the season. He talked about his wife and kids all the time, how much he missed them, and what he wanted to do when he retired. For a young guy, he talked a lot about retiring. He wanted to build shopping centers and malls in Ohio. Back in the 1970s, a lot of malls got built, but the area around Canton, roughly between Cleveland and Columbus, where Thurman was from, still didn't have much except brutally good high school football teams.

When Thurman arrived as starting catcher in 1970, the Yankees rose to a higher level than at any previous time in my career. We won 93 games and finished second. Except for Thurman, the team wasn't all that different from the few years before. He was the quickest catcher I'd ever seen. The first game I saw him catch, he threw out an attempted base-stealer. I never saw the ball leave his hand! He got rid of the ball like a second baseman turning the double play. It barely touched his glove. I'd never seen that before.

The man was fearless. There are about a dozen films and videos of Thurman getting creamed at the plate and showing the ump how he held the ball. "He had a brilliant baseball mind and was as tough as they come," Hecht agrees. "He hurt his arm in 1974 and played hurt all year because the team was finally contending. His arm was never the same after that, even with his quick release."

He had confidence at the plate, too. He was a line-drive machine. In fact, our hitting philosophies were pretty similar, so we talked hitting a lot. For instance, he would say, "I just can't see him," about Tigers lefty Mickey Lolich. He was a big guy, of course, but he had a kind of funky delivery, dipping down, what they call, "throwing out of his shirtsleeves." I hit Mickey well. If you look at the record, you will find that Thurman hit him pretty well, too. But he didn't think he did, or he thought he should have been even better.

The guy we hated the most was Mike Cuellar in Baltimore. He threw a lefty screwball—slow, slower, and slowest. You'd be waiting, waiting, waiting, and finally when you thought you had waited long enough, he'd come inside with his pathetic 80-mile-per-hour fastball, and it looked like Nolan Ryan's! It would saw your bat off. We hated him. Just about the only hit I got off him was in an old-timers' game. He pitched like an old timer when he was playing, so I was ready for him. My bat had finally slowed down enough that I could time his annoying screwball.

Thurman loved playing for the Yankees, and no one loved winning more than he did. He was actually a calming and very important influence when the clubhouse got a little crazy during the well-documented Reggie-Billy-George years. His well-constructed façade protected not only him, but in a way, the whole club. He kept focused on what was happening on that field, and that helped everyone.

"He was crazy, but he was a leader," remembers Ron Blomberg, Thurman's roommate for four years. "The catcher *should* be a leader, but a lot of them aren't. He'd get in your face if you didn't hustle. In the heat of battle, there was no one better."

It wasn't always a battle, thankfully. "We played basketball together in the off-season, and he and his wife often went out with my wife and me," Ron says. "It wasn't like today, when the players all go their separate ways. Thurman was, however, the worst dresser on the team. Wait. He was the worst dresser in the league.

Maybe in all of baseball. I know it was the 1970s, with all the poly-ester, so none of us looked that good, but Thurman was a Goodwill reject. He also didn't shave. A lot of the guys didn't shave sometimes, like Piniella, but Munson was the only one who looked like a derelict. Man, we had some good times."

Sometimes Thurman did things on the field that you just thought were impossible for him. In the third game of the American League playoffs, after George Brett had hit three solo homers off Catfish Hunter and Gossage, of all people, had blown a lead in the eighth, I singled and Munson came up against Doug Bird. "He hit one out of the park at the deepest part of Death Valley, in left center," Henry says. "It was at least 450 feet. At *least*. I said to myself, 'How can he do that? He can't do that. He can't hit a ball that far.' But he just did. That's what the great ones do. They do things they *can't* do."

For the record, I hit a homer in the sixth inning of the fourth and final game against Dennis Leonard, to win for Ron Guidry, 2–1. Okay, so it didn't go 450 feet, but it still counted.

The Ohio boy always lived inside Thurman, and I don't think he ever felt comfortable in New York. Certainly he never brought his family east. He wanted to fly jets so he could get back there even quicker, even more frequently.

A lot of people think that Thurman didn't like Reggie Jackson or that they didn't get along. Baseball writer Henry Hecht believes it is deeper than that. "At first Reggie's presence was threatening to him," Henry says. "But finally they came to get along well. In fact, he even invited Reggie to accompany him on that last flight. Reggie had a previous commitment and couldn't go."

When we found out about his death, well, I don't remember too much about that day. It was a terrible day for all of us. Mr. Steinbrenner flew the whole team out to Ohio on his private jet. I don't remember much about that, either. It was all just a very sad, very dark time for me.

I don't remember what Bobby Murcer said in his eulogy, either. I do remember the first game we played when we returned. We were playing a home game against the Orioles and Dennis

Martinez. Bobby was hitting second, playing left. We had gotten only four hits off Martinez and were behind 4–0 in the bottom of the seventh. We looked about as beat as a team without its captain would look. Then, with two out, Bucky Dent walked, Willie Randolph doubled, and Bobby put one over the fence. 4–3. Then, in the ninth, Dent and Willie got on again, and Bobby singled them both in, a walk-off single, if you will, and we won 5–4, with Murcer driving in all five. A true ballplayer's eulogy.

We were hurting inside, but we won the game. That just about defines what Thurman Munson was all about.

chapter 2

Welcome to the Show

These five men, pictured here before an old timers' game on August 3, 1974, epitomize the Yankees "show." From left are Mickey Mantle, Yogi Berra, Whitey Ford, Joe DiMaggio, and Casey Stengel.

The Peril of Top Billing

Whitey Ford had won more than 200 games and had established a reputation as one of the all-time clutch pitchers by the time I came to the Yankees, and Mel Stottlemyre was just getting started. The connection between them has been central to Yankees pitching for more than 50 years.

Whitey's 9–1 record as a 21-year-old in 1950 was followed by eight and two-thirds innings of no earned runs in the Series-clinching game against the Phillies. He arrived at Yankee Stadium with the body of a kid and the brain of a seasoned veteran. He continued his excellence until the day he put down his glove in 1967. He passed his way of getting the job done to Stottlemyre.

Like Whitey, Mel came to the big club during a season when the pennant was not being placed at the feet of the Yankees by divine providence. They had to work for it very hard. Also like Whitey, Stottlemyre arrived pitching like a veteran. He hurled a complete-game win against the White Sox in his first start, in mid-August 1964; beat Baltimore, going eight and two-thirds in his second start; and shut out the Red Sox at Fenway Park his third.

Most very young pitchers who find major-league success do so with tremendous stuff, usually a fastball that takes a few months for hitters to see. Both Mel and Whitey, though throwing hard enough, won more with their brains than with their arms.

In 1964 Mel was a rookie, but Whitey was still a good pitcher, going 17–6. He was also a new pitching coach, hired by new manager Yogi Berra. Casey always called Yogi his "manager on the field." Now Berra was getting a chance to manage from the dugout.

"I liked coaching," Whitey remembers. "I had great pitching coaches like Jim Turner and Johnny Sain, who knew how pitchers liked to be treated. I tried to treat them the same way."

What Mel and Whitey shared was the ability to let hitters get themselves out. "The main thing I could do, that a lot of guys didn't or couldn't, was throw a curveball for a strike on 2–0," Whitey says. On 2-0, most hitters figure a pitcher needs a strike. They guess *fastball* and screw themselves into the ground swinging at the curve. As a kid, I had to laugh when I'd see Whitey make lefties like Jim Gentile look like Little Leaguers on the Game of the Week. It was like hitters never learned. Whitey Ford would throw you any pitch at any time. "Once I got them thinking about a breaking pitch, I could slip a little fastball past a guy on 1-2," Ford says. The hitter was so far behind it made Ford look like Bob Feller. Mel pitched the same way, because he could get all his pitches over any time.

Mel was dominant in 1964. He won nine of his 12 starts, with an earned-run average of just more than 2.00. Because the Yankees won the pennant by a game over Chicago and two over Baltimore, clearly they were also-rans without him. It was clear that Mel would be the future ace, following Whitey. Nobody knew he would do it so soon.

Whitey started the first game of the Series against St. Louis but was unable to hold a 4-2 lead in the sixth inning. His arm was gone for the rest of the series and had only one more full season in it. Mel started the second game and won 8-3, going all the way. He left the fifth game after seven against Bob Gibson, pitching him to a standoff, only to see the bullpen lose in the tenth. Then, as a 22-year-old rookie on short rest, he faced Gibson again in the final game. He lost, but by the end of the season, everybody in baseball knew that the Yankees had a new ace, probably for many years.

He lasted 11 years, all good ones, but retired after the 1974 season, at age 32, with what we now know is a rotator-cuff injury. Today, he would miss a year and then come back for who knows how many more. Less than a year after Mel retired, Tommy John had his famous surgery and was able to pitch another 14 years. Mel deserved to be part of our winning teams in 1977 and 1978, much in the way that Don Mattingly deserved to be part of the Joe Torre-era champions.

Yet Mel was an integral part of Torre's success. His first year as Yankees pitching coach was 1996, the first of Torre's four ring years. It was the second time Mel led a pitching staff to ultimate victory, serving as pitching coach for the Mets during their 1986 championship. It was Mel who encouraged Andy Pettitte and David Cone not to be afraid to throw the breaking ball on 2–0. And so, the legacy from Whitey to Mel endured more than 50 years.

Exactly when did Mel take over from Whitey as Yankees ace? Maybe when Whitey was unable to continue in the World Series. But it might have come even earlier.

On September 22, 1964, the Yankees had a doubleheader in Cleveland. They held only a one-game lead over Baltimore, two over Chicago. Sonny Siebert was starting the first game for Cleveland, Dick Donovan the second.

"I went to Mel and told him he was starting the first game, and I'd start the second," Whitey recalls. "Mel was very happy to start the first game. He was all smiling and everything." It meant a lot to a rookie to start the first game. But they didn't call Whitey "Slick" for nothing.

Siebert was a rookie like Mel. A little *too* like Mel, in fact. He started the season in the Indians bullpen but was so impressive that he landed in the starting rotation and had been very effective. Donovan, on the other hand, was winding down a good career. He was an above-average pitcher for the 1950s White Sox, got knocked around a few years, and resurfaced as the league's earned-run leader of 1961 and a 20-game winner the following year.

But he had struggled since. Worse, three weeks earlier he pitched his heart out, and possibly his arm, when he lost to the White Sox 3–2. He pitched into the thirteenth inning, yielding 16 hits. He lost on a bunt single, a stolen base, another bunt single, and a sacrifice fly. Since then he had not started a game and had given up four runs in three innings of relief.

So, while Whitey was boosting Mel's young ego, he was *really* saying, "You pitch against the young stud, and I'll pitch against the old man who just croaked his arm."

As it turned out, the Yankees swept the doubleheader and eventually won the pennant. Mel won 5–3, thanks to homers by Joe Pepitone and Roger Maris, but he had to pitch his heart out in a close game against Siebert. Meanwhile, Whitey got an early lead against Donovan and breezed home, 8–1. Donovan won exactly one more game in his professional career.

Mel got the ego boost. Whitey got the easy win.

Words to Live By

Not all the best athletes, and certainly not all of my best friends, found their ways into the big leagues. Ian Dixon threw as hard as anybody as a schoolboy pitcher in Vancouver, British Columbia. In spring training one year, the room in which he lived housed players who combined for 164 major-league victories. Mel Stottlemyre won 164. Ian Dixon won zero.

As a Canadian, Ian didn't get to play nearly as many games as I did growing up in California. The weather worked against him, and, until Toronto Blue Jays executive Pat Gillick started working on it in the 1970s, there weren't many good organized amateur leagues for kids and potential pros. The most famous Canadian major-league name, if not the best player, when Ian was growing up, was probably George Selkirk. Actually, Selkirk was more famous for having replaced Babe Ruth in right field for the Yankees than for anything he accomplished once he got there.

Ian threw so hard so young that he tried out for the Vancouver Mounties, a Triple A franchise in the Pacific Coast League, at age 15. He didn't make the team, but by the time he finished high school, every team in the major leagues knew his name. What Canadians lacked in game experiences, they made up for in other areas.

For instance, a team could sign a Canadian without it counting as a draft pick, the way teams today sign so many very young Latin American players. Even more critical in those times, Canadian young men were not subject to a military draft, which interrupted many major-league careers, including mine, and thwarted others completely.

Ian signed with the Yankees for $45,000, though he probably could have gotten more from other teams. But his dad, who had played semi-pro baseball in Quebec, was a Yankees fan, and, because they were also the elite team at the time, they had the edge.

Ian played a bit later the same year that he graduated from high school, 1961, which was the same year I finished at Centennial High in Compton. I waited until the following spring to get started, but he was sent to a rookie league in Kentucky. They saw that he had a great arm and could hit, so "Ian Dixon pitching prospect" became "Ian Dixon, brand-new third baseman."

I flew to spring training from Los Angeles, while Ian drove his pride and joy, a red and white Chevrolet Impala convertible, with white top and white sidewalls, purchased with a portion of his bonus money. To guys right out of high school like us, it was about the prettiest and coolest thing we could imagine. We met at lunch our first day there.

At the end of the spring, you had to look on the bulletin board to see what team you were on. Nobody told you. We got the shock of our lives when Ian and I saw we had both been assigned to the same team. It was Greensboro, Class B, a lot higher than we expected.

That year the Yankees let all their minor-league managers pick their rosters. Vern Rapp was the Greensboro manager and must have liked what he saw. We thought we would be going to Class D, Idaho Falls. Greensboro was a much tougher league and a lot tougher town. At least, it was for us.

We were still teenagers and were a bit naïve. Growing up black in Los Angeles, I certainly knew about racism, but I had never been exposed to the Southern variety. Ian, as a Canadian, had not either. We rode north together in his Impala, leaving Florida and heading toward Greensboro. One day, we were driving through Georgia with the top down. It didn't take many looks from the locals to understand that was not a good idea. Later, I had to hunker down in the back seat while Ian went inside roadside diners for food for both of us. That march through Georgia is what forged a friendship that has lasted more than 40 years.

When we arrived in Greensboro, things were no better. Blacks could only sit in right field, and the bathrooms at the park were segregated. Worse, we might have been in good shape, but neither of us was prepared for Carolina League pitching. We were soon driving back down to Florida. The park, the lights, and the culture were so much better for us in Fort Lauderdale, it hardly seemed like we were being demoted.

It was a pitcher's league, but there were a lot of players who would last. Besides Mel and Mike Hegan and I on the Yankees farm, Tony La Russa, Lou Piniella, Jim Wynn, and Bert Campaneris were there, among others. Ian played third, and I played second. We won the pennant.

The following year, I found my way to Greensboro on my own and solved the pitching problem this time. I was on my way. It didn't work that way for Ian. In some ways, having such a strong arm worked against him. They first made him a third baseman, but he sometimes mopped up an inning here or there on the mound. Some of the coaches liked what they saw and thought he would be better off as a pitcher. Or not. Or then again maybe he would. If this sounds confusing, imagine how it felt to Ian.

While he was being switched back and forth, he wasn't really advancing in the Yankees minor-league system. But yet they wouldn't release him to sign with another team, because they thought he still might develop. This was at a time when all the major-league teams were cutting back on their minor-league operations.

While the big leagues were expanding, the minors were contracting. The Yankees system cut back from nine teams to five. So, in one year you had the same number of players competing for about half as many jobs. It was common to read magazine stories titled "Are the Minor Leagues Dead?"

Moreover, there was no money to be made playing in the minors, and, at the time, not that much in the majors, unless you were a star. Ian, though only 21, felt like he was running out of time. He was, in terms of one of the options that were still on his table: a college athletic scholarship. He accepted a basketball scholarship to the University of British Columbia, which led to a career as a financial advisor. It is safe to say that, although Ian never made the majors as a baseball player, he became a major-league financial advisor.

I stayed at his beautiful home overlooking the Strait of Georgia the year I coached for the Vancouver team in the Oakland A's organization. The Strait of Georgia was much more hospitable to both of us than the state of Georgia was when we were traveling through it as young men.

While being shuttled from pitcher to third, Ian naturally looked for guidance wherever he could find it. One day in spring training about 1963, Ian was playing third in one of those split-squad games, where the players in camp get divided into more than one team so everybody can play. Stars and scrubs, prospects and suspects, all get mixed together. That's why Ian was playing third and Whitey Ford was pitching. It was against the Baltimore Orioles.

Now, Ian was still a kid who didn't need spring training to get in shape. He was eager to play every day, anywhere. But Whitey, who was a veteran in his mid-thirties with a couple thousand innings behind him, needed every minute. Yet I suspect he wasn't that thrilled to be spending a sunny day in Florida pitching to kids and retreads.

The Birds had a hot prospect named Paul Blair, who was a big star at Los Angeles' Industrial High School at the same time I was playing in Compton. I'd heard he was good, but to me, the main rival I had in high school was Ron Woods. Although I thought I did well to hit about .400 in high school, Ron hit about .600! Who hits .600, in any league?

I believe Ron would have been a big star, but he suffered a severe beaning in his second year in the minors. He made it to the show, and we were even Yankees teammates in 1969 and 1970, but he never was able to use the ability we saw in him back in high school.

The Mets had signed Blair before they had even played a game, but they left him unprotected from the minor league draft, and the O's grabbed him. In that split-squad game, he dragged a bunt down the first-base line for a single in his first at-bat. Next time, he hit a hot liner down the right-field line for a double. Now, Whitey was tiring, and he called timeout and called Ian over. *Wow, Whitey Ford wants to talk to me!* Ian remembers thinking. *Now I'm going to get something that will really help me. This may be the key that puts me in the majors,* Ian thought. *I'm going to get the distilled wisdom of one of the smartest, craftiest pitchers in history.*

Whitey put his glove over his mouth and told Ian, "I ain't got shit today, kid. Try not to get hurt." Words to live by.

Throw Strikes and Keep 'Em Low

Al Downing was a fine young pitcher in Trenton, New Jersey. He finished high school in 1960 and joined a local All-Star team good enough to compete in the National Baseball Congress tournament in Wichita, Kansas. At the time, the NBC was about as important as the College World Series is today. College ball wasn't very big then, so many of the best prospects used Wichita as a showcase for their skills. Also, a lot of corporations and local businesses sponsored teams. As kids, Billy Martin and Whitey Herzog were just two of the players who got signed after excelling there.

As college baseball became more important, many teams were composed of collegians playing in their off-seasons. In 1969, for instance, Chris Chambliss was the NBC Most Valuable Player, moonlighting from college with a team from Alaska.

It was a big deal to go to the NBC tournament, especially if you were the best pitcher in town and you were barely out of high school. So, 18-year-old Al Downing took the mound against a local team, the Wichita Weller Construction Company. He looked out at the opposing pitcher, looked twice, and still he didn't believe who he was seeing.

Who was Al pitching against that day? Satchel Paige!

Satch was 50-something, his true birthdate as unknown then as today. But he wasn't that removed from the professional ranks. He last pitched in the major leagues with the St. Louis Browns in

Al Downing, shown here before a Yankees game in 1961, got the surprise of his life when he found himself pitching against the iconic Satchel Paige in the 1960 National Baseball Congress tournament in Wichita, Kansas. Photo courtesy of Getty Images.

1953. He relieved in 53 games and started four, pitching more than 100 innings. His earned-run average of 3.53 was well below league average. He was fourth in the league in saves. It appears he could have pitched longer in the majors. He did pitch longer, going back to Triple A with the International League team in Miami, where he continued as an effective reliever for a few more years.

As late as 1965, Charlie Finley brought him back as a publicity stunt to pitch three innings when he was, more or less, 58. The Red Sox didn't score against him. Carl Yastrzemski, with a double, got the only hit. Considering the guys who were pitching regularly for Kansas City at the time, Satch should have started more.

One of the reasons for Paige's longevity was that, during all those years of pitching, he used his brain at least as much as his arm. Ted Williams, who thought more about hitting than anybody else in the history of the human race, told this story about facing Satch in his major-league "rookie" year of 1948. At the time, Williams was on his way to hitting .369. He walked 126 times and struck out only 41, once against Paige. Williams never forgot it.

"His first pitch was a dinky little fastball just a little too far inside," Ted would tell anyone who he thought knew enough about hitting to understand the moral of the story. "I pulled it foul down the right-field line, way up into the stands. The next pitch was just a little faster and caught a little bit more of the plate. Damned if I wasn't a little early on that one, too, and pulled it foul. So he's got me 0–2. He winds up, and I see, at the top of his motion, his wrist is turned just a little bit. It's a curveball grip.

"So I wait for that breaking pitch, and Satch throws another one of his goddamn little fastballs right down the middle, and, like an idiot, I'm caught looking, way too late to swing.

"There is only one runway from both dugouts into the locker rooms, so both teams go down there together after the game. I'm walking down, and Satch comes up next to me and says, real quiet-like, 'Don't try to think with ole Satch.'"

Paige's fastball might have broken a pane of glass, but probably not a storm window. The moral of the story: don't try to think with ole Satch. That is, no matter how smart you think you are, there might just be somebody else out there who is thinking, too.

Paige wasn't only a publicity stunt in 1960; he was also still something of a pitcher. He defeated young Al Downing, going five or six innings. "We were in awe of him," Al remembers. "I'd tell guys later in the summer, and they'd say, 'You pitched against *who*?!'" Al might as well have told them he faced Babe Ruth or that Ty Cobb stole a base on him.

Al might not have been as surprised to see Paige if he had known the history of the tournament. It originated in the early 1930s. By 1935 it had aspirations of expanding from a local event to a national tournament. To attract attention, it invited Satchel Paige's touring team to compete. It won the championship, with Paige winning four games and striking out 60 batters, which is still the tournament record. Knowing the legend of Satchel Paige, it wasn't all that surprising that he would show up again nearly 25 years later!

After his game, Downing spotted Paige relaxing in the stands, watching another. He summoned the courage to speak to him. Al remembers that Paige said to him, "You're a fine pitcher. Keep it up." That puffed out Al's chest for about the next six months. He then asked the old master what, exactly, was the secret of good pitching?

"Keep the ball low, son," he said. "And throw strikes."

In December 1960, Al Downing signed with the Yankees. Prospects who signed in the spring after school usually went to Class C or D, the lowest classifications back then. Al started spring training with the Binghamton, New York, Class A team, which was a pretty high place to begin.

"1961 was an expansion year," Al says. "The Yankees had a number of pitchers taken by the other teams, not just at the major-league level, but at every level. Even if they weren't that thin on New York's roster, they didn't have the depth in Triple A or Double A they once had, and that trickled down, so there was room in Single A for me." They were also trying to determine how advanced he was as a pitcher. Al assumed, as everyone else did, that he would soon be sent to a lower classification.

The Binghamton team trained in Bartow, Florida. It's right in the very middle of Florida and is named after the first Confederate officer to be killed in the Civil War. What else do you need to know? "I had never spent any time in the South before. There were only three black players on the team," Al says. And one of them was Puerto Rican Elvio Jimenez, who wasn't even truly black. Elvio's lifetime major-league batting average is .333. He went 2-for-6 on the last day of the season in 1964 and was never higher than Triple A Toledo afterward.

In spring training 1961, Elvio and Al were not allowed to live with the other players, instead bunking with private black families. "That's when I learned of the great cooperation and sense of community among the black people in the South," Al says fondly. "I stayed with the McCoy family. It was a great cultural education for me. Everybody back then really worked to make sure it would be better for their kids than they had it. And everybody knew the answer was education."

Jimmy Gleeson was the Binghamton manager. He spent a few years in the majors in the 1930s and 1940s. He also played for the Triple A Newark Bears when he was probably good enough to play in the majors. The Bears were the top Yankees farm team, where good but not great players, like Gleeson, were stockpiled. This was common before free agency. "Gleeson treated us very well," Al says. "He always asked how we were getting along. He knew it was hard for us. He cared about us."

"One day he asked how I was feeling. I said fine, and he told me to pitch some batting practice," Al recalls. "Then he put me into a game against the Tigers' Class A team in Lakeland. I pitched five good innings, and he started me against the same team the next weekend."

"I like you," Gleeson said. "You throw strikes." Satchel would have been proud.

"Then I pitched against the Yankees' Double A team, Amarillo," Al says. "They had Pepitone, who hit out of a deep crouch, like

Stan Musial. Everybody was talking about how far he could hit a ball, but he looked kind of funny to me, in that exaggerated crouch. I threw him a fastball on the fists, and he just cleared it out of there. I mean, he hammered it. It's been almost 50 years, and Joe Pepitone reminds me every time I see him that he hit a homer off me the first time he saw me. I did pretty well against the rest of the lineup, and then Jimmy started me against the Yankees' Triple A team from Richmond. Tom Tresh was their big star."

After that, Gleeson told Downing, "I'm taking you with me. You have to prove to me that you can't pitch."

"So I started the season with Binghamton. Our first game is in Springfield, Massachusetts, and it's April, and it's snowing!" Al says. "Back then, in the minors, there was no set pitching rotation. The manager would just put a ball on the stool in front of a pitcher's locker, and he started. So it's Opening Day, and the ground crew is shoveling snow off the field, and the ball is on my stool! I thought somebody was playing a joke on me."

"Nope," Gleeson said. "You got it today."

"So I went out and pitched a three- or four-hit shutout," Al remembers proudly. "And everybody started saying I was lying about my age!" I'm glad I didn't get my first look at a young Al Downing fastball when it was cold enough to snow! Al never did prove to Jimmy Gleeson that he couldn't pitch. He went 9–1 with about a strikeout per inning and an earned-run average of 1.84.

One day Jimmy came up to Al after a win and congratulated him. "I thought maybe he was going to tell me I made the All-Star team or something," Al says.

Gleeson said, "You've been called up." Al figured he might have been promoted to Amarillo or Richmond, but no. He was called up to the Yankees.

"I thought somebody was kidding me," Al says. "Now I think maybe they didn't want to send a black player to Texas or Virginia. The Yankees hadn't had too many black players yet."

Back in the 1940s, Branch Rickey had acquired minor-league teams in Toronto and Nashua, New Hampshire, at least partly because he wanted a place for black players to progress relatively free of racial problems. Jackie Robinson started in Toronto, and Roy Campanella and Don Newcombe started in Nashua. It was 14 years since Robinson came to the National League, and the Yankees *still* hadn't given this much thought.

On July 19, 1961, Al Downing made his major-league debut, starting the second game of a doubleheader against the expansion Washington Senators in old Griffith Stadium. He got the side in order in the first, striking out Chuck Hinton and Jim King. Then in the second, he forgot Satchel's advice: single, walk, walk, hit batter, walk, shower. Hal Reniff came in and allowed a single by pitcher Dick Donovan, followed by an error by usually sure-handed third baseman Clete Boyer. Al was charged with five runs and finished the day with a major-league record of 0–1. He appeared in four more games in relief but mostly had a ringside seat as the 1961 Yankees became one of baseball's legendary teams.

The next year, he pitched well for Triple A Richmond, spending the whole season there, except for a one-inning Yankees appearance at the end of September. He struck out more than a batter per inning but walked almost as many. When a young pitcher with as much stuff as Downing walks so many, it is usually because he doesn't trust his stuff. He figures that he needs to throw as hard as he can all the time or is afraid to challenge the hitters. He's forgetting Satch's rule.

Downing made 10 starts in Richmond at the beginning of 1963. He was still striking out a lot of batters and still walking too many. But a funny thing happened when he was called up to the big club in June. His strikeout rate stayed high, but his walk rate plummeted. He walked a lot more batters in the minors that he did in the majors! Chalk it up to experience, courage, whatever. Suddenly his fastball was missing bats a whole lot more than it was missing the plate.

He pitched one inning in relief, then shut out those same Senators on two hits, striking out nine. He finished 13–5. He had double figures in strikeouts eight times in 22 starts, with a high of 14 against Cleveland. He pitched four shutouts and lost the second game of the World Series to Johnny Podres and the Dodgers, 4–1. He was 22.

He was the first African American to pitch for the New York Yankees. He learned how to throw strikes and keep 'em low, just like Satchel Paige advised.

A Yankees Rebel

Jake Gibbs wasn't just an All-American quarterback for the University of Mississippi Rebels. He was *the* All-American quarterback. His teams from 1958–1960 had a record of 29–3–1.

His timing was also excellent. The new American Football League was beginning to challenge the older NFL by offering big contracts to top college players. Jake was drafted by the Cleveland Browns and the Houston Oilers. The Browns were still looking for the true successor to Otto Graham. The Oilers had a good but aging quarterback in George Blanda, so Jake was in a great bargaining position. In fact, he was offered $105,000—by the New York Yankees.

A few months after he was voted Most Valuable Player in the Sugar Bowl, he was in the Yankees dugout shaking hands with Mantle, Ford, Berra, and the rest. It surprised a lot of people but not the people who really knew Jake Gibbs.

"I always enjoyed baseball more," Jake, who still lives in Oxford, Mississippi, and who was voted into the College Football Hall of Fame in 1995, says. "It was more relaxed. I had been playing baseball longer. It was my first love. My college coach told me that I could probably have gotten as big a bonus from football, with the bidding wars and all, but my dream was baseball. Plus, I figured I'd have a longer career in baseball, because it was safer, with fewer injuries."

At the time, the signing looked like a classic case of the rich getting richer. The Yankees were the dominant team in baseball, on their way to one of their best seasons. In May 1961 Jake flew to New York and spent a few days with the team, then accompanied them on a short road trip. "I felt nervous at first, but all the guys gave me a great welcome," Jake remembers. "There was a tradition on the Yankees of not hazing rookies but welcoming them. The veterans showed the rookies the right way to do things. I felt right away that they were not only good players but good human beings, and that feeling has lasted through the years."

Mickey Mantle, in particular, made him feel at home. Perhaps it was because he recognized in Gibbs a country boy like himself. Mantle knew how strange New York could seem and went out of his way to help the rookie fit in. They became good friends. Jake still has an autographed photo of Mantle inscribed, "To Ole Country."

There was even a fellow Rebel on the team. Jack Reed had also played both football and baseball at Ole Miss. Jack and Jake later roomed together in 1964 on the Yankees' Triple A farm team in Richmond, after Jack lost his reserve outfield job. Younger players, such as Tom Tresh and Joe Pepitone, could handle both infield and outfield.

Jake saw Richmond soon enough, as he was sent there after his taste of a big-league locker room and greeting from the Yankees stars. Still, starting a professional baseball career in Triple A was a testament to what the Yankees thought about their new catcher, who they hoped would follow in the great Yankees catching tradition: Dickey, Berra, Howard, and now Gibbs.

His first big-league games came the next year: two brief appearances late in September. In both, he scored as a pinch-runner. In his first, he ran for Elston Howard and scored on a Berra sacrifice fly. In the his second, he ran for Hector Lopez, and in the ninth he scored one of four runs the Yankees used to come back to beat the Senators 8–5. He stayed in the game for the bottom of the ninth, replacing Clete Boyer, who had been replaced in the top of the inning. It was Jake's first big-league appearance on defense and, strangely enough, his only appearance at third base.

He had to wait another year for his first official at-bats and his first hits, going 2-for-8 at the end of 1963. "I was only in New York very briefly those years, and Bobby Richardson and Steve Hamilton let me stay with them," Jake says. "Later, I lived in several places in Bergen Country, New Jersey." One of them was Teaneck, which must have had some special appeal to catchers, as Yogi Berra and Elston Howard also lived there at various times in their careers.

In many ways 1964 was a repeat of the previous year. Jake Gibbs played all year at Triple A and then came north for a short taste of the big leagues. But this year Jake was scheduled to be added to the World Series roster if the Yankees won the pennant. They clinched on the final weekend, and Jake was looking forward to his first World Series, even though he had started only one game in his big-league career.

He started his second on October 4, 1964, the last game of the season. It was against the Indians and Luis Tiant. Manager Yogi Berra, saving his pitching staff, started Jim Bouton but let him pitch only three innings. Several other hurlers followed, none for more than two innings until Stan Williams went the last five. It was a successful strategy, and the game was tied 1–1 from the third inning through to the thirteenth! Young Jake was getting a workout.

Vic Davalillo led off the thirteenth. He was 0–5. He swung and barely made contact. The ball glanced off Jake. More precisely, it glanced off his bare hand. It hurt, but Jake was a tough guy. He had been knocked around by some of the best college linemen in the nation. He stayed in the game.

Davalillo, no fool, knew that Gibbs was hurt. On the next pitch, he bunted for a base hit. With one out, Fred Whitfield singled Vic to third. By now, Jake knew something was wrong. Staying in the game was impossible. Johnny Blanchard came in from right field to catch. Leon Wagner grounded to short, Davalillo scored, and soon the game was a 2–1 Yankees loss. It was an even bigger loss for Jake Gibbs.

His finger was broken. Another rookie, Mike Hegan, who was also fresh off the farm, replaced Jake for the World Series and made brief appearances in three games.

Jake recovered completely in the off-season and came to the Yankees to stay in 1965, completing his entire major-league career as a Yankee in 1971. Neither he nor the Yankees ever got close to another World Series during those years. Certainly this is not what anyone suspected when Jake Gibbs, the famous college quarterback, chose his first love—baseball—at least partly because he thought it would be safer, and got handshakes all around in the Yankees clubhouse in 1961.

chapter 3
End of an Era

Whitey Ford attributes his Hall of Fame induction to Yankees pitching coach Johnny Sain, shown here in 1961. Sain was the Yankees pitching coach from 1961 to 1963, and those were the best years of Ford's career.

When the Wheels Fell Off

Before even one pitch was thrown in the 2008 Yankees spring training, Hank Steinbrenner, who had just taken over daily over-sight of the team from his father, George, was quoted in *The New York Times* about his team's pitching, saying, "It's going to be strong for the next 10 years."

He was referring to three top pitching prospects—Phil Hughes, Joba Chamberlain, and Ian Kennedy—who, going into the 2008 season, had collectively pitched a total of 116 innings and won eight games. In 2008 their combined record was 4–11.

There may be no longer shot in sports than the odds of a young, hard-throwing pitcher, no matter how highly regarded, completely fulfilling his potential. Hank's confidence, if not his hope and enthusiasm, might be dampened if he were to reflect on his team's fortunes of some 40 years ago.

Al Downing, after showing so much promise at such a young age, came down with arm miseries midway through the 1965 season, when he was only 24. "One night I just had a kind of burning in my elbow," Al recalls. "Elston Howard said, 'We won't throw the hard, quick curve, just the big curve.'" Al could survive without the quick-breaking curve, but he couldn't dominate.

The burning elbow came and went over the next few years, limiting Al's starts, innings, and effectiveness compared to his per-formance his first two years. Of course, he wasn't the only Yankee who suffered in 1965, which is known as "the year of the Yankee collapse," when the wheels fell off a team that had gone to the seventh game of the World Series and won five consecutive American League titles. They finished sixth, 25 games behind the Twins, the first time they lost more than they won since 1925.

"If they had the medical care back then [that] they have now, it wouldn't have been so bad," Downing surmises. "Ford and Mantle both had surgery after the 1964 season." Neither per-formed up to his career standards afterward.

"We had an exhibition game down in Puerto Rico," Al remem-bers. "They had a full house, and we had traveled so far, they didn't want to call it off when it started to rain. Elston was catching, and when he stepped forward to throw out a base runner, his foot slipped and he threw awkwardly. He heard his elbow go 'pop.'" He continued as the Yankees' primary catcher for two more years, but he never hit the same again.

His catching career was kind of backward, in a way. A great catching talent who was stalled behind Yogi Berra, Elston had to find playing time in the outfield and at first base. He never caught as many as 100 games in a season until he was 32. Then he caught 129 games, then 132 games, and then, in 1964 when Yogi was the manager, 146 at age 35! Since Yogi caught 140 or more games per season for five years, he probably didn't think much about it, though he never caught that many after the age of 30, and at 35 he caught only 63. It wasn't surprising that Elston's body broke down.

"Tony Kubek hurt his neck taking a bat out of the rack, of all things, and Roger Maris, after a bad hamstring injury ruined his year in 1963, broke his hand in 1965," Al says. "Yankee management thought Maris was dogging it, then they found out his hand was broken." Roger, never sold on the way he was treated in New York, resented this terribly. He never hit with power after the hand was broken but was happy to leave the city when he was traded to St. Louis, where he helped the Cardinals to two pennants.

Whitey Ford's and Al's arm problems were not the only ones. Ralph Terry, after being the staff workhorse in 1962–1963, got a sore arm before he was 30 and was traded to Cleveland. Bill Stafford, who was only two years older than Downing, came down with a terminal rotator-cuff injury in 1963, after winning 14 games during each of the two previous years.

Stan Williams, a young, fireballing Dodger, was brought over at the cost of Moose Skowron. He went 10–13 in his two years in pinstripes, first suffering arm trouble, then, on the last day of the 1964 season in the same game against Cleveland when a Vic Davalillo foul broke Jake Gibbs' finger, he was also hurt badly. A hard-sliding former Michigan State running back–turned-outfielder named Al

Luplow messed up Williams' knee so badly on a play at the plate that he pitched exactly four innings the following year.

Of a planned rotation of Bill Stafford, Mel Stottlemyre, Jim Bouton, Al Downing, and Ralph Terry, only Mel survived career-ending or -threatening injury. He made it through 11 years before his rotator cuff was shredded.

Bouton was supposed to take a place in the rotation for many years after winning 21 games in 1963. Al remembers, "He held out that winter and came to spring training late. He tried to prove he could pitch with a short spring training, and I think it hurt him. Bouton and I both suffered from a Yankee prejudice of wanting pitchers who were six feet or taller."

This prejudice has increased and spread to other teams over the years, but it is particularly strange for the Yankees, whose best pitcher of all time is the 5'10" Whitey Ford. Luis Arroyo, who made a living saving games for Ford, was two inches shorter. Of course, in my day Ron Guidry dominated from less than six feet, and Bobby Shantz was a useful Yankees pitcher for several years at 5'6", leading the league in earned-run average in 1957. Obviously, I am also a good argument against having a height minimum for anything in baseball!

"I never felt overworked or sore," Bouton says. "I just wanted to pitch as much as they'd let me. I never thought I was burning out. I'm sure I pitched many games throwing 120–130 or more pitches. Now, though, I think pitch-counts are a good idea, especially for the smaller guys like Pedro Martinez. It's a wonder his arm is still connected to his shoulder."

By the time I came up, Bouton was already hurt, but I remember him as a maximum-effort guy with every pitch. He threw beyond overhand. Everybody who saw him remembers that he often knocked his hat off, his arm came so far overhand. He was kind of weird about his arm, even by pitchers' standards. He wouldn't sleep on his right side and was really careful about keeping it covered.

"I did baby my arm. I figured a concert pianist doesn't do carpentry," Bouton reasons. "In 1965 I felt a toothache in my bicep early in the season. At first I didn't think it was serious, because it wasn't in the elbow or shoulder. By midseason I couldn't pour a glass of milk from a carton. That's when I knew I was in trouble.

"One of the reasons I didn't pay more attention to it sooner was that 1964 started the same way. I had some soreness and started poorly, but it came around. We all thought it would come around again, but this time pitching just made it worse," Bouton laments. "The brachialis muscle, which connects to the ulna and the humerus, gave me chronic pain. I lost the elasticity in the arm and never got it back. I had to go with the knuckler."

The brachialis muscle controls the rotation of the lower arm. No rotation, no movement on the ball. No movement, no career. The knuckleball, which requires no rotation, was his only hope.

After struggling to stay healthy, Jim was let go to the legendary Seattle Pilots in the expansion draft, which was the backdrop to much of his famous book, *Ball Four*.

The first time I faced him, when he pitched the ninth inning of a 5–4 Yankees win in Seattle, I was hitting cleanup and doubled. He said it was a hanging knuckler. A hanging knuckler? What the heck is a hanging knuckler? I thought they *all* hung!

Like Bouton's, Downing's arm just kept getting weaker. Sometimes it was better, sometimes worse. His record for 1965 shows a steady, if slightly downward, trajectory. "The injury was never really diagnosed," Downing says. "It bothers me even today. It is a problem with the ulna nerve. The pain flows from the nerve all the way down my arm and into my second and third fingers. Sometimes it was hard even to grip the ball." No wonder the Al Downing fastball that brought him to the majors at age 20 became a memory.

Everybody knew some changes had to be made in the off-season. Ralph Houk, who had been everybody's favorite manager, was now the general manager. He was no longer everybody's favorite. Within two weeks, he had traded both Roger Maris and Clete Boyer. He got Charley Smith and Bill Robinson in return, to replace them in right and at third.

Charley didn't work out at all. Bill turned into a fine hitter and outfielder, helping his team to a World Series victory. Unfortunately for Houk, it wasn't the Yankees, but the Pirates in 1979. He had come to New York as damaged goods, his injured right arm hurting him both in the field and at the plate.

There was a fine athlete available to take over center field, left field, shortstop, and third base. Unfortunately, it was just one player: Tom Tresh. He was able and willing to play just about anywhere, but of course, he couldn't play everywhere. The shuttling back and forth might have hurt his career, but not nearly so much as a pair of bad knees, which gave him something in common with Mantle, in addition to switch-hitting.

Houk returned as field manager in early 1966, after the team began 4–16. They were only seven games under .500 the rest of the season, but they could not overcome the awful start and finished 10th. The team's performance was a shock to fans and a shock to the players. "In going from pennant winners to also-rans, we found out there was no magic in the Yankee insignia or pinstripes," Bouton recalls. "You had to do it on the field. Just putting on the Yankee uniform didn't make you great."

The following August, the now-weak-hitting Elston Howard was traded to Boston for two pitchers who contributed little. Al believes this hurt the Yankees far more than just losing a catcher who hit .196. "When Ellie left, Jake Gibbs took over and had no one to help him, no veteran to teach him. Howard could have backed up Gibbs and helped him a lot. Instead, he helped the Red Sox win the pennant. That hurt." Yogi Berra famously said that Yankees catching great Bill Dickey "learned me all his experience." Yogi helped Elston so much they remained friends all their lives. But Jake's backup was Frank Fernandez, who was five years younger, greener, and whose main claim to fame is that he finished his career with more walks than hits.

"The sale of the Yankees to CBS hurt," Al believes. "Many scouts left. The Yankees used to sign the best of all the players, until the draft began. Then they only got one shot for a really prime prospect, and they didn't have the scouts to draft well. They got complacent, didn't change with the times. They got way behind signing blacks and Latin [Americans]. We'd see Dick Allen and Tony Oliva and wonder when we were gonna get some of these guys to help us.

"They didn't do such a good job of player development, either. Those minor-league teams in the early '60s that Roy was on had a lot of talent. But except for Roy and a couple of others, they didn't make it. Why? They almost lost Roy. They loaned him to the Dodgers, and it wasn't until the Dodgers wanted him that the Yankees thought they better keep him."

In 1969 Al started only two games until August. From then until the end of the season, he started 13 games, completed five, and went 6–2. "There was this big rush to pitch me in August," Al recalls. It wasn't because of a pennant race. Though the Yankees improved to only one game under .500, this was still only good enough for fifth in the new division format of six teams making up the American League East. "They were showcasing me. It was time for me to leave," Al says. He went to Oakland. The Yankees received Danny Cater, whom they later traded for Sparky Lyle, in one of the biggest steals in the history of baseball. Not a bad return for a young but arm-weary southpaw.

"Oakland was happy to have me, but they were loaded with young talent, as we all discovered just a few years later," Al recalls. "So I went to the new Milwaukee club, which had been the Seattle Pilots. They were going nowhere, and Frank Lane became their general manager."

Frank "Trader" Lane invoked fear and loathing from most players, as he would trade any player at any time. He lost his job in St. Louis for suggesting the Cards trade Stan Musial for Robin Roberts. He traumatized a generation of Cleveland Indians fans by trading Rocky Colavito. But Al remembers him as a general manager who respected him. "He came to me and said, 'We have a lot of kids. Where do you want to go, the Cardinals or Dodgers?' I told him the Dodgers, because I liked the West Coast. Two days later I was in Los Angeles. Lane respected that I had some seniority. I always remembered that."

The four-man rotation of Al Downing, Don Sutton, Claude Osteen, and Bill Singer started all but 20 games in 1971, in which the Dodgers lost the Western Division to the Giants by one game. Al tied with Tom Seaver and Steve Carlton with 20 wins, trailing only Fergie Jenkins' 24. Yet Al is unimpressed.

"I didn't pitch any better than the previous year, when I was 5–13," Al insists. "The key to having a good pitching record is having a good team behind you." Having a team that catches and hits the ball does wonders for a won-and-lost record. Winning 20 games did, many years later, qualify Al for admission to a very exclusive club, the Black Aces.

Founded by Mudcat Grant, its membership is limited to African American pitchers who have won 20 games or more. There are a total of 13 members, the most recent addition being Dontrelle Willis, who was added in 2005. "It is to recognize black pitchers and also to encourage young black athletes to continue in baseball," Al says. "We also help raise money. One year we went down to Smokey Joe Williams' hometown of Seguin, Texas, outside of San Antonio, to help raise money for his memorial scholarship fund."

Williams, whose father was African American and mother was a Comanche Native American, is considered the greatest black pitcher of all time, excepting, perhaps, Satchel Paige. Even Ty Cobb, that notorious racist, said that, had Williams been allowed in the big leagues, he would have won 30 games a year.

"Maybe we ought to change the rules," Al says. "Last year C.C. Sabathia won 19 but won the Cy Young Award." With five-man rotations the norm today, 20-game winners are near extinction.

Al Downing's bad ulnar nerve was just one of many reasons the Yankees were on the way down when I came up. It took a long time to rise again, but we did it. I know Al was among the happiest former Yankees to see me finally get a ring. He knew what it had been like for me because he saw the good Yankees times and the bad.

A Sain Path to the Hall of Fame

Whitey Ford started one of my first big-league games, in September 1965, the month I was called up. He pitched 10 full innings, losing 4–3 on a two-run homer by Norm Cash in the top of the tenth. This was one of only two career homers Norm had off Whitey, who usually hit Ford terribly and often got the day off when he pitched. I played right field but went 0-for-3. Tom Tresh drove in all three runs. He was the only hitter with more than a loud foul off Mickey Lolich that day.

It was that kind of year for Whitey in 1965. In 1964 he was 17–6 *and* the pitching coach for Yogi Berra, in the last pennant year for those great teams. The next year, new manager Johnny Keane brought in his own pitching coach, Cot Deal. Whitey returned to being a player only and pitched almost exactly as he had the year before. Without being supported in the style to which he had become accustomed, his record was only 16–13, still not bad on a sixth-place club that finished 25 games out. In any year, when you took the field and Whitey Ford was on the mound, you knew you were a Yankee.

The next two years, Whitey again pitched well but not often, and, as the Yankees continued to slide, he added only four wins to his career total of 236. He retired at age 38, though he had been pitching spectacularly in the big leagues since he was 21, when he got everybody's attention by going 9–1. "Everything began to hurt," Whitey says.

It wasn't just his arm that had been worn down considerably, though. He developed a blood clot in his golden left shoulder. He had it removed and pitched again, but then the rest of his body refused to cooperate. He was lucky, though he didn't think so at the time. A similar clot in the right shoulder of Astros Pitcher J.R. Richard, having gone undiagnosed, caused a stroke, ending his career at age 30 in 1980. A blood clot in the left shoulder has to take the local lane to get to the heart. The right shoulder takes the express.

By the time I took right field in Whitey's defense, everybody knew he was going to the Hall of Fame. Yet Whitey himself believes that his ticket to the Hall was punched by one person: Johnny Sain. Sain was pitching coach for the Yankees for only three years. Those three years, 1961–1963, were the best of Whitey's career.

"With Casey I pitched, at most, every fifth day. Sometimes he would hold me back even longer, six days or more, so he could have me pitch in a specific park or against a specific team or pitcher," Whitey says. Stengel's moves produced eye-popping win percentages for Ford, and, because the Yankees were winning the pennant almost every year, it's hard to argue against the strategy. But pitching excellence was measured by winning 20 games, and Whitey is correct when he says, "It is hard to win 20 when you are only starting 30." Under Casey, he got as high as 19 wins, but only once.

This changed when Ralph Houk replaced Stengel in 1961 and hired Sain as his pitching coach. Sain had only one year of big-league coaching experience, and that was for a bad team in Kansas City. Houk and Sain knew each other well from their years in the Yankees bullpen, when Johnny was finishing his career as an effective jack-of-all-trades starter and reliever for Casey and Houk was a third-string catcher watching Yogi catch 140 or more games a year. During that time, Ralph discovered what many baseball people eventually learned: Johnny Sain was one smart son of a gun.

In the October 1961 issue of *Sport* magazine, Ralph described to writer Fred Katz how he came to hire Sain. "We were together as players for three years, 1951–53, with the Yankees. Sitting in the bullpen and watching him work with other pitchers was almost like watching a laboratory experiment. We talked a lot about mound patterns and theories and agreed practically on everything. I said to myself then that if I ever got to manage a major league team, Sain would be my pitching coach."

How smart was Sain? If we think about pitching as math, most pitchers approach it as though they were adding or subtracting. Some get as far as long division. Johnny Sain was doing calculus, figuring the algorithms on how far a sinker dropped, while the rest of baseball was arguing whether a curveball really curved. A huge number of players name Ralph Houk as their favorite manager they ever played for, and an even higher percentage of pitchers came to revere Coach Sain.

Sain's approach to Ford was deceptively simple: let him pitch. Ford remembers, "He let me pitch every fourth day, no matter who it was against or where it was." For the next three years, Whitey averaged 38 starts and 22 wins, twice leading the league in wins. To this day, Ford believes these three years allowed him to attain the gaudy stats, which Stengel's more convoluted approach had denied him, and pushed him over the top for the Hall of Fame.

The added work didn't bother Whitey. "I was never the fastest pitcher. I was fast enough, but I relied more on different breaking pitches," he says. "I also stayed ahead on the count, so I never had to throw that many pitches. It would have been tougher if I was one of those hard throwers who had trouble finding the plate."

In fact, Sain and Ford were similar pitchers. Both played around a lot with different grips, knowing that a slight difference in the way a ball is held will cause a slight difference in the way the ball comes across the plate. This small difference determines whether a batter connects squarely or dribbles a disappointing grounder back to the mound.

It was not necessary to pitch like Sain to be helped by him. Buddy Daley, who pitched for Johnny both in Kansas City and New York, says he owes his big-league career to him. It was Johnny who first put the lefty in a major-league starting rotation. "No one had the confidence in me that Sain had—not even myself," Daley told Katz in the *Sport* magazine piece.

"Sain doesn't teach by example and say, 'Now, son, this is the way I did it, and I want you to do it the same way.' He picks out the strong points of each man and works from there. What helps make John such a great coach is that he wasn't a pitcher with just one good or great pitch. Instead, he could throw everything well, and so he can be of help to every type of pitcher. What's more, he treats each pitcher as an individual."

Besides Ford and Daley, Sain helped young and old arms on that fabled 1961 Yankees team. Aging Luis Arroyo, who had been up and down for years, had his best year. Why? "Until Sain got hold of me, my screwball didn't break as much as it does now," Arroyo told *Sport*.

Gangly Rollie Sheldon came from nowhere or, more precisely, from Class D, to win 11 games for the Yankees in 1961. He said, "Sain started me from scratch in spring training. We worked on the basic fundamentals, and he wouldn't take anything for granted. That's where I learned my change-up. But he didn't do it by saying, 'This is the only way it's done.' He showed me three or four ways of throwing it and let me pick the one I liked."

Jim Kaat, who came to the Yankees late in his career as a reliever and stayed for many years in the broadcast booth, benefited from Sain's coaching in the mid-1960s with Minnesota and again in the 1970s with the White Sox. He says, "Johnny always tried to represent ideas that would help you improve. He didn't have a set method. He could really teach pitchers how to make the ball do different things with grip pressure and spin." Two of Kaat's 20-win seasons came with Sain in Chicago, and his biggest year, 1966 (when he won 25), came the year after Sain finished tutoring him for two years with the Twins.

Success followed Sain. After he left the Yankees, he helped the Twins to the 1965 pennant, then the Tigers to their 1968 flag. He helped Chicago get close, then, after a few years off, came back to Atlanta in 1985 and 1986. Those Braves teams didn't win, but getting 17 and 14 wins out of Rick Mahler might have been more of an accomplishment than getting 20 out of Whitey Ford.

It is easy to see how Sain developed his pitching philosophy. He averaged 273 innings his first five full years in the majors and won more than 20 games four of those years, after losing three prime early years to military service in World War II. The Yankees traded a young pitcher named Lew Burdette for Sain for the stretch run of 1951. Although Burdette later exacted revenge by beating New York three games in the 1957 World Series, Sain's ability to start or relieve helped Stengel to three of his five consecutive World Series wins from 1949–1953.

One way Sain got so smart as a pitching coach, as I'm sure he would have agreed, was to have once been stupid as a pitcher, at least once. In the 1948 World Series, Sain started out as good as a pitcher can be, beating Bob Feller 1–0. Sain's Boston Braves lost the next two games, so it was up to him to pull them even in Game 4. He was behind 1–0 in the third inning with Larry Doby at bat, two out, and nobody on.

"I threw him a helluva change-up; he swung like he had never seen one before," Sain would say to anyone who would listen, using his folly as a teaching moment. "So I threw him another one. Same result. So I thought, *well, this is easy.*" Doby hit the third change-up out of the park, for a 2–0 lead. The Indians held on to win 2–1, led the series 3–1, and won it all in six. To his dying day, Johnny Sain believed throwing three off-speed pitches in a row to Larry Doby cost the Boston Braves the World Series.

"*Do not* throw the same pitch three times in a row!" Sain would orate. "I don't care how good a pitch it is. I don't care who's at bat. The third time the batter sees it, it's not a good pitch anymore." Then he would tell his sad story of that third pitch to Doby.

An off-speed pitch isn't off by the third time a batter sees it.

Whitey Ford probably would have gone into the Hall of Fame if Don Rickles had been the Yankees pitching coach in 1961–1963. But don't suggest this to Whitey, who knows how much Sain helped him, just as he helped Jim Kaat and countless others. Sain knew the best way to get smart was to learn something after being stupid.

Major Changes

Jim Bouton's arm was already hurt when I came up, so I remember him as a guy who struggled to find his way back to the

Jim Bouton (right) is shown in 1963 with Al Downing (center) and Whitey Ford. Bouton's hurt pitching arm was one of many injuries that plagued the Yankees in the mid-to-late 1960s, causing the team's performance to suffer.

success he had before his arm snapped. He was the type of guy who would take the opposite side of any argument. He could argue both sides. The old-guard players and coaches didn't like that. I don't know if he really believed what he said or not. I think he was a bit of what you might call a contrarian.

"I disagree that I was a contrarian," Bouton says today. "I really did disagree with most players on most issues back then: politics, women, race, just about everything, you name it. If you had heard most of their opinions, you would have disagreed, too. In a normal world, rather than the dugout and locker room, *they* would have been considered contrarian."

His opinion is also a little contrarian, or perhaps more precisely, a little deeper, on why the Yankees took such a nosedive in 1965 and 1966, after decades of success. Sure, there were injuries and age, but he believes another factor made a big difference, too. "We had the wrong manager," he says. "Johnny Keane was a nice man, a very religious man," Bouton says of the manager who replaced Yogi Berra after beating the Yankees with the Cardinals in the 1964 World Series. "The Cards were a straitlaced organization, no longer the Gas House Gang."

The Yankees of the 1960s were closer to those old Cardinals of the 1930s. "The Yankees were a partying team," Jim recalls. "Out all night, lots of drinking. Ralph Houk was the right manager for us then, and Yogi, too. Yogi just let us play. If you were too hung over to play, he let you sleep it off until you could. A lot of people don't know it, but we liked Yogi as a manager." The Yankees players were not happy to see him fired and were even less happy when the new guy was the manager who had just defeated them.

"Early in spring training, Keane saw our general way of behaving, and he didn't know what to do," Bouton says. "It was like hiring Billy Graham to manage the Hell's Angels. It wasn't that he was a bad manager. It was a bad fit."

Bouton says, "Houk was my favorite manager." In fact, if you ask all the men who played under Ralph Houk—for the Yankees, Tigers, or Red Sox—an amazingly high number of them will name the man they all called "the Major" as their favorite manager. Bouton says Houk was "an excellent, wonderful guy. It wasn't that he was such a brilliant manager, but he knew how to stay out of the way of a good team. He was more of a handler of men than a strategist. But that's what you need in baseball. Patience. Not getting too high or too low."

Fans might think it odd to hear Houk described as a man of patience who didn't get too high or too low, as he was seen any number of times throwing very animated and vociferous temper tantrums at umpires back in the days when it was much more common. In fact, it was just another way of taking heat off his players, defending them. In that way, he was very much like Joe Torre, though their outward demeanors could not have been more different.

Houk replaced Casey Stengel at the end of the 1960 season, when, according to Casey, the most successful Yankees manager made the mistake of turning 70. He also made the mistake of losing the World Series to what most considered an inferior Pittsburgh Pirates team.

Houk was then considered the best young managerial candidate in baseball, having piloted the Yankees' Triple A team in Denver to three successful seasons and acted as a coach with the big club for three years. Similarly to the way they thought of Joe Girardi in 2007, Yankees ownership thought that if they didn't get their guy now, he would lose patience and bolt to another team. Two World Series victories followed, then a pennant-winning team that got swept, but perhaps excusably so, by the likes of Sandy Koufax and Don Drysdale.

Meanwhile, the team was sold to the CBS network just after an important decision had been made. Houk was promoted to general manager. He was certainly familiar with being promoted, because he had acquired his nickname through field promotions from private to major at the Battle of the Bulge and Bastogne in World War II. Houk always said about his officer's rank, "My main qualification for promotion was being able to stay alive." This works well in both baseball and the corporate world.

Houk soon began to illustrate what is known as the Peter Principle in business. That is, "In a hierarchy, every employee tends to rise to his level of incompetence." The particular skills that made Houk a good field manager did not translate well at all into being a general manager, whose job, then as now, is to negotiate players' contracts.

"In the days before free agency, it was the GM's job to take unfair advantage of the players and pay them as little as possible," Bouton explains. "It was a nasty role. General managers sometimes received bonuses based on the amount of money the team saved on payroll. Houk was all 'podner' this and 'podner' that as a manager. We didn't buy his 'podner' stuff as GM"

It is well documented that Houk and CBS decided to fire Yogi before the end of 1964. Then Yogi embarrassed them by being such a bad manger that he won the pennant in an exciting race and extended the World Series to its final game. Bringing in Keane seemed, even to little kids who were Yankees fans, stupid and cruel.

"Mantle and I arrived late for a game almost at the start of the 1965 season," Joe Pepitone recalls. "Keane starts yelling at us, 'Get out there! Get out there!' meaning, get on the field. You can't talk to Mantle like that. Not after what he had given to the club. Keane was a Jekyll and Hyde. He was nice as could be off the field. On the field and in the clubhouse, he tried to be some kind of by-the-book hard guy. It didn't go over. Finally, I couldn't take it anymore. I just got lost for two days, jumped the team. It was Houk that found me and got me back in shape to play. I told him, 'I can't play for that guy anymore.' I was glad Houk came back. Bringing in Keane was a bad move for everyone."

After a terrible 4–16 start in 1966, the team let Keane go. Houk returned to the dugout. His natural personality just didn't take to the hard line needed to be a general manager. Another corporate decision was made that seemed logical on the surface: a manager who was promoted didn't work out, so return him to his old job, where he had performed well. Except it didn't work out that way. "Those Yankee teams that once loved him now resented him after he spent a few seasons trying to screw them out of as much money as possible," Bouton says. "Those teams weren't *that* bad. They just quit on him.

"The new guys that came up for the first time in those years, like Roy, Bobby Murcer, and the others didn't remember him as the general manager," Bouton says, "and he was all *podner* again."

It was a little confusing when I first came to the Yankees at the end of 1965. I had never played anything other than the infield, not even in high school. One day, Keane comes up to me and says, "How about you taking a couple of fly balls in the outfield in practice today? I might use you out there sometime, just to get you in the lineup."

I said sure and went out to shag a couple of flies. I went back into the locker room to get dressed, and when I saw the lineup card, there I was, starting in right field! I was ready to have a heart attack. So the first game I ever played in the outfield was in the major leagues.

One of the reasons he used me out there, at least at first, was that he was using Bobby Murcer at shortstop, and he didn't want to start two rookies in the infield. Even though we were out of the pennant race, some of the teams we played were still in it, and there was an unwritten rule that you didn't play too many rookies together in the lineup against contending teams. If Keane played a completely rookie double-play combination, other teams might think we were conducting tryouts rather than trying to win. It doesn't happen as much today.

But, yes, Houk was my favorite manager, too. He settled me in the outfield, finally, in 1968. I started 1967 at third, one of a number of players who proved not to be Clete Boyer. He said, "This year you are going to be just in the outfield, so don't even think about the infield anymore." This was a relief, because up to then I'd been switching around, and the team never told me what it might want next.

Houk gave you a lot of rope to hang yourself. We were afraid to cross him. We were afraid he would break you in two if he got angry. He still had the reputation as a real tough guy, left over from the war. I always felt Ralph stuck with me for a few years when I was struggling, trying to find my place in the major leagues. He kept seeing something in me. Eventually, I started getting the hits everybody thought I should be getting, but other managers might have given up on me or traded me.

Sam McDowell was at the end of his career and played for Houk only one year, 1973, but he wishes it had been more. "He got the best out of you. He would sit down and talk to you on the bench or in the clubhouse," Sam recalls. You might think that all managers would do this; it is so simple and obvious. But many don't, leaving you to wonder what you might have done differently or better, with no idea how to improve.

"When I was with Cleveland I thought he was just a pat-'em-on-the-back, get-along-with-everybody type, but he was smart; wise, in fact," Sam says. "He knew how to get into your head and your heart without you knowing it. He would tell you little things, things you never thought about, that really helped you. He was smart enough to know the smartest guys don't go around showing off how smart they are all the time."

Even Joe Pepitone, who is not known for being too high on authority figures, thought very highly of the Major. "Houk was great," Joe says. "The most important thing a manager does is handle men. He knew who to pat on the ass and who to kick in the ass. He knew how to handle everybody. He was like a father to me."

It was Houk who moved Joe to first. "I played center field all through the minors," Joe says. "But we had Mantle, Maris, and Tresh. So I moved to first, and they traded Moose Skowron." Later, when Joe moved back to center for a few games or a year, some people were surprised, because few players in baseball history who were first basemen were good enough on defense to handle center field. They didn't know we had a center fielder playing first base all along.

"Houk was amazing," Joe says. "I hit about nine homers in spring training of 1963, and the writers were asking Ralph how he thought I might do for the season. He said, 'Joe ought to hit about .270 or .280, with maybe 27 or 28 homers, drive in 90 or so.' I ended the season hitting .271 with 27 homers and 89 RBIs." Houk couldn't predict the future, but he knew his players, which is sometimes just as good.

Over the years, Houk, this supposedly hard-bitten war veteran who just let the veterans play and stayed out of their way, earned a deserved reputation for developing young players like me. After he left the Yankees, he took over a terrible Tigers team; developed rookies such as Alan Trammell, Lou Whitaker, Lance Parrish, and Jack Morris; and left them to win the World Series under Sparky Anderson in 1984.

Even later, with the Red Sox, he helped many of the young players who were on their pennant winner in 1986, including Wade Boggs, Marty Barrett, and a rotation of fine young starting pitchers: Roger Clemens, Bruce Hurst, Bob Ojeda, Al Nipper, and Oil Can Boyd.

Meanwhile, Jim Bouton is now developing new ways to market vintage baseball; that is, baseball the way it was played in the 19th century. His organization helps organize teams, leagues, and special events with a historical flavor, for town centennials and the like. Of course, Jim Bouton does it his way. His teams don't play according to any specific year but use rules that combine what he believes to be the best of several years.

This outrages the orthodox vintage reenactors, who consider his approach akin to reenacting Civil War battles with armies dressed in red and green, firing both M-16s and crossbows. Once again, Jim Bouton is a contrarian.

He would probably disagree.

chapter 4
Keeping It Real

Roy White is congratulated by Roger Maris after hitting a home run in 1966. Maris hated the spotlight and wanted only to be recognized by his teammates as a fine all-around player. Photo courtesy of Roy White.

Pepitone Circles the Bases

Legend has it that Joe Pepitone spent all this bonus money before he even attended his first professional spring training. I don't know if he spent it all, but Joe is very specific about where a fair chunk of the money went. He says he spent it on "a 1958 Thunderbird. That was the first year it was a four-seater. It was black with a red interior. And side exhaust pipes."

Spring training in various Southern towns was pretty weird for me, sometimes scary, but the Yankees' Double A farm team at Amarillo was an equally new and challenging experience for Pepitone, an Italian boy from Brooklyn. "I played center field, as I did all through the minors," Joe says. "Amarillo is a big cattle town. There was a slaughterhouse right beyond center field. I could hardly stand the stench. Let's just say there were a few times I left my lunch in center field."

Stomach distress was a continuing problem for Joe in the Texas League. "We had 20-hour bus rides between those Texas towns. And then, for a month later in the season, we flew to Mexico to play teams down there," Joe recalls. "These weren't major-league Mexican town, but smaller cities like Puebla and Matamoros. They seemed pretty strange and backward to us. Our team warned us not to eat the food. Instead, they made us stuff like cheese sandwiches. Cheese sandwiches from Amarillo."

Joe was leading the league in hitting. Or, more precisely, his roommate, Phil Linz, and he went back and forth in the lead, both around .325. "We were walking down some street in Mexico, and we see this little pushcart," Joe says. "I say to Phil, 'I'm starving, We gotta get something to eat.' Phil reminds me that we were told not to eat the food."

Joe Pepitone is not known for always doing what he was told. "I ordered a burrito, and so did Phil. He took one bite, gagged, and spit his out. I ate the whole thing in about 10 seconds," Joe says. "During the next few days I must have lost 30 pounds." The burrito was not, to say the least, good for Joe's digestion. Or his batting average.

"That damned burrito cost me the batting title," Joe laments. Phil, keeping his strength, finished at .349 and won the title. Joe finished at .316 and couldn't wait to get back to some good Brooklyn Italian food.

The following year, both Joe and Phil were in New York. "The Yankees always tried to put rookies' lockers next to veterans. Mine was next to Mantle's. He was a great guy, a great teammate. I'd hit a home run, and the writers would crowd around my locker, and he'd yell, 'Why do you want to talk to the rookie? You should be talking to me,'" Joe remembers. Mickey made Joe smile by pretending to be jealous.

"Yes, I was the first major leaguer to bring a hairdryer into the clubhouse. I also was the first to wear a Nehru jacket," Joe says. For those of you old enough to remember Nehru jackets, you will know this qualifies as a dubious achievement. If you don't know what a Nehru jacket is, consider yourself among the fortunate. It is like a suit jacket, but instead of lapels it has a standup collar and buttons all the way up. Why? To better display your love beads, of course!

"When the other guys saw that dryer, believe me, I was called every name you can think of and a few you might not know," Joe says. "I'm blowing my hair, and everybody is looking at me. The next day Mantle puts baby power in my dryer. I'm wearing a blue suit and turn the dryer on. The next day, Mantle comes into the clubhouse and heads for the whirlpool. Because of all his leg injuries, that's the first thing he did every day. He gets in, turns it on, and I sneak up behind him and pour a bottle of Joy into the water. In about five seconds, Mantle turns into one huge bubble, and the room is full of bubbles. He jumps out yelling, 'I'll kill you, you big-nosed SOB!' But by the time he got to me, he was laughing. Mantle was a regular guy and a funny guy, just a good ole country boy." Mantle loved playing jokes and telling jokes. He must have known a million jokes, some of which were even funny.

Mantle was more than a jokester. He was a good friend to Joe. "After my divorce, I was living with my mother in Brooklyn, and Mickey invited me to live with him," Joe remembers. "He lived in a two-bedroom suite at the St. Moritz on Central Park South." It was a little bit different than Joe's mother's place.

"Yes, we had fun," Joe says, which one can assume is an understatement. "He taught me some new ways to have fun. I taught him a few new ones, too."

Joe went to Houston after the 1969 season in one of several trades that didn't work out too well for the Yankees. Then halfway through 1970, he was sold to the Cubs. "I never hit .300 until I went to the National League," Joe says. "The American League had a high strike zone. Pitchers threw a lot of curves and change-ups." American League umpires back then wore those huge inflatable chest protectors. They couldn't crouch too low, and it caused a higher strike zone than in the National League, where umps wore protectors similar to catchers. "National League pitchers threw lower and more fastballs, sliders. I loved to hit low fastballs. I loved hitting in the National League."

With the Cubs, his manager was a kindred spirit, Leo Durocher. "He was my kind of manager. He didn't care what you did last night as long as you gave 100 percent the next game. He made playing fun," Joe says. "One night we were all over at Frank Sinatra's. Leo left, and I wanted to stay. Leo just said, 'You can stay, but you better hit tomorrow.'"

Leo directed everything that his team did on the field, but sometimes his players reacted more than necessary. Joe says, "Johnny Callison was in right field one day. He was a real nervous, shy type of player. Leo drove him nuts. He was in and out of the lineup from day to day. He was never certain of what Leo wanted from him. One day it starts to rain a little, and puddles are starting to form along the edge of the dugout. Guys might slip when they run into the dugout, so Leo has a towel, and he's swinging the towel around, mopping up these little puddles.

"Callison thinks Leo is using the towel to position him in right field," Joe laughs. "Leo swings the towel a few times one way, and Callison is almost on the right-field line. Then he swings it the other way, and Johnny's all but in the center fielder's lap. The guys on the bench see what's happening, but naturally everybody shuts up. At the end of the inning, poor John comes into the dugout and says to Leo, 'Geez, Leo, make up your mind. Where in the hell do you want me to play?' Leo didn't know what in the heck he was talking about, and everybody falls off the bench laughing."

Joe has played for some powerful personalities, from Houk and Durocher to, of all people, Donald Trump. In the 1990s Joe took the field between games of a Yankees doubleheader as a member of the Donald Trump All-Stars, in a charity game versus a team of actors and musicians. Joe was prepared to hit the big grapefruit.

"I played professional softball on the Trenton Statesmen in the American Professional Softball League," Joe says. That was in 1978. There was almost no money, but there was a lot of fun, and Joe learned how to pump those slow pitches out of the park.

But now Joe was pushing 50. "Trump needed some players, and I said okay. Naturally, I expected to play first base. I take the field at Yankee Stadium wearing my old Yankee uniform, and Donald says, 'You're playing shortstop.'"

Joe said, "I play first."

The Donald replied, "No, I play first. That's my position. It's my team. We need a shortstop." So Joe went to shortstop.

"Of course, the first batter hits a weak grounder to me at shortstop," Joe says. "I'm left-handed, so I charge in, glove it, and have to turn my body completely around to make the throw, and I throw it into the dirt. Guess what? Trump digs it out, makes a pretty good play. In fact, he wasn't a bad first baseman at all. Turns out he played there quite a bit as a kid. I'm not saying he could have been a pro, but he was good. Anyway, he did pretty well in real estate."

Joe eventually did his Derek Jeter imitation. "Oh, yeah," Joe adds. "I won the game with an inside-the-park home run." He hit the ball a very long way to right center, showing that among the actors and real-estate moguls, there was one guy out there who hit 219 major-league home runs, made three All-Star teams, and won three Gold Gloves at first. Joe would have preferred hitting the ball over the fence. "I thought I was going to have a heart attack between second and third."

It was another game-winning home run that includes Joe's all-time favorite baseball memory. Joe won the sixth game of the 1964 World Series with a grand-slam home run in the eighth inning. Cardinals manager Johnny Keane pulled knuckleballer Barney Schultz with the bases loaded and two outs, putting in a lefty, Gordon Richardson, to face the lefty-swinging Pepitone. Richardson was a lefty relief specialist before they became anywhere near as common as they are today.

"The first two pitches were the same pitch, hard sliders," Joe remembers clearly. He hit two foul balls. "*Darn*, I'm thinking, *I should have hit those.* On the next pitch, I was so focused on the ball, I didn't know where I hit it. It went off the right-field roof, but I was running so hard, I almost passed the runner on first. Coming home, there was Mickey, waiting for me with open arms." Mantle had been walked intentionally earlier in the inning and was on third for Joe's homer. "That was my biggest thrill in baseball. Not hitting the grand slam to win the game, but having Mickey waiting for me at the plate, smiling."

The Baseball God at the End of the Bench

My first big-league experience was at the end of the 1965 season, a reward for a season in the Southern League that earned me its Most Valuable Player Award. I hit .333 in 42 at-bats in New York, but I was under no illusion that this was going to be easy. The next year I hit more than 100 points less and found my way back to the minors for a time.

Sitting in the Yankees dugout with Whitey Ford, Mickey Mantle, Bobby Richardson, Cletis Boyer, and a lot of other players I knew better from the backs of their baseball cards than from the locker room was pretty heady stuff. I was only 21. The rookies tried to act cool, but it wasn't easy. I once played in the Mickey

Mantle League when I was a kid back in Compton, and now I was playing with Mantle.

Although Mickey had this huge aura and was a total fan favorite by the time I arrived, I was always surprised by how little-appreciated Roger Maris seemed to be, both by the fans and the front office. Sure, Yankees fans would have preferred that their old favorite, Mantle, break Ruth's home-run record, rather than Maris. And although they more or less rooted for Roger in the following years, there was no love there.

Personally, I found him to be a great guy. He treated me with respect as a rookie and was always nice to me. He was smooth in the outfield, with a very accurate arm. He could easily handle center field, and, when Mickey's legs demanded it, he did.

In 1966 he was criticized for half the season because of a hand injury. Some of the New York press accused him of malingering. Later, we all found out he had a broken hand. That was the last straw for Roger. He intended to retire rather than come back to a town that thought he didn't play hard. Gussie Busch in St. Louis enticed him to the Cardinals with one thing the Yankees could not offer: a Budweiser distributorship. I'm sure the beer earned Roger far more money throughout his life than all the homers he hit.

The hand still bothered him in St. Louis, limiting him to 14 homers and 100 RBIs over two years, but he played an excellent right field and helped the Cards to two pennants while the Yankees were heading downhill.

If Roger was all too human, then Mickey, regardless of the adulation the rest of us gave him, was, too. Getting to know your hero is often something different than one anticipates, as my buddy Arturo (Art) Lopez discovered. Art—with Bobby Murcer, Rich Beck, and I—all joined the team in September 1965, a reward for good minor-league seasons.

"Back in those days, Mantle wasn't just what you'd call a superstar now; he was a god," Art remembers. Most rookies looked upon the vets, and especially Mantle, with such awe that we almost never spoke to them. For the most part, they didn't have much to say to us, either. Put that together with the lousy year the Yankees were having in 1965, the first time they were really out of the pennant race since, well, ever, as far as we knew, and you had a dugout that could be a little tense, a little quiet. Johnny Keane, the Yankees manager in 1965 and early in 1966, contributed with a demeanor that was not unkind but that created about as many laughs as a country deacon.

"I had a great relationship with Mantle, though," Art says. "He knew I was little older and treated me with a little more equality than the younger rookies." Mantle would also never let on that Lopez was older than the Yankees management assumed. There is a lot that goes into being a good teammate.

It was the middle of September, and a huge crowd gathered in Yankee Stadium, even though both our team and the visiting Tigers were far out of the pennant race. Arturo and I took our usual places on the bench, and soon back-to-back doubles and a homer by Buddy Barker gave us a lead, which we had trouble holding.

Except for the three hits we got that inning, we managed only one more the rest of the game against starter Joe Sparma, John Hiller, and, pitching the final three innings, a young kid with scary stuff, who came out of nowhere to win 16, Denny McLain. Bobby Murcer helped write his ticket to the outfield that day with two errors at shortstop, neither of which contributed to unearned runs, but both still made the day just that much more frustrating.

So when Mickey took three high fastballs from Sparma and sat down, he was in no mood for further irritations. As Mantle returned to the dugout, for some reason Ross Moschitto, another rookie, was standing right in front of the bat rack. "Ross was an amazing physical specimen," Art says, "but he had the knack for being in the wrong place at the wrong time. Mantle approached the bat rack, glared at Ross, and said, 'Get the f*ck out of the way.'"

For all I know, Ross wrote home that night, "Mantle spoke to me," but the effect on the dugout was chilling. Believe me, everybody on the bench began to get real busy cleaning their nails or watching the next batter and just generally trying to avoid Mantle's gaze or getting in his way. "I'm at the very end of the bench, looking the other way and trying not to get involved with his anger," Art says. "The next thing I know I feel this big push against me. Mantle slams his body right next to mine."

There was silence. Then, "Hey, Arturo, you know how Yuma, Arizona, got its name?"

"Ah, no, Mick," Art replied.

"A guy robs a bank down there," Mickey explains. "A policeman comes by, sees a black guy outside the bank, assumes he's the robber, and shoots him. Just before he dies, the black guy looks at the cop and says, 'You mo....'" Mantle fell into Lopez's lap like he'd been shot. The baseball god was dying in his arms; symbolically, of course.

Johnny Keane looked down toward them, and everybody was trying hard not to laugh, like junior high kids exchanging naughty jokes.

Two hours later, given Bobby's two errors, Johnny brought in Tony Kubek, the sure-handed veteran, to play short. With one out, Tony booted Mickey Stanley's grounder. Jerry Lumpe singled him to second, and he scored on a Norm Cash hit. Tigers won 4–3 in 10 innings. For the final eight innings, our entire offense was a Hector Lopez pinch single. Little wonder Johnny Keane did not become known for his sense of humor.

Vietnam Happened

Bobby Murcer and Dooley Womack. Roy White and Rich Beck. What links these names together? They share a Topps 1966 Rookie Stars baseball card. On the back of the Beck/White card, it says of Rich, "A 25-year-old right-hander with lots of potential." Our collective major-league career was 1,884 games—1,881 for me, three for Rich. What happened to that potential? Vietnam happened.

There has always been a close connection between baseball and war, from players' careers being truncated by war to players doing their part to entertain the troops. Here Joe DiMaggio signs autographs and chats with GIs stationed at an advisory team compound near Ben Hoa, 18 miles northwest of Saigon, on November 17, 1969.

Military service has been a factor in baseball for generations. There are accounts of Civil War soldiers on both sides playing baseball before and after battles. Hall of Fame pitcher Christy Mathewson died at age 45 of a respiratory illness caused by poison gas he was exposed to during training in World War I.

World War II baseball is well documented. Many stars lost years to the war effort. By 1945, almost the entire prewar rosters of most big-league teams were in service. Although no baseball stars were killed in action, we will never know if any potential stars were. For instance, had D-Day gone a bit differently, we might never have heard of Yogi Berra, who had played only one year in the minors before the war.

Yogi was on a navy rocket-launcher off the coast of Normandy on D-Day. He was mesmerized by the sight of the explosions around him. "It was like the Fourth of July," Yogi remembers. He also remembers his commanding officer telling him to get his head down. Yogi ranks that officer high among the people responsible for his career. Had it not been for that officer, Yogi might not have gotten his head down in time.

Don Newcombe, Willie Mays, and Whitey Ford, to name just a few, lost prime years during the Korean War. Tony Kubek was called to active duty in 1962, paving the way for rookie Tom Tresh to play shortstop for the Yankees until Tony returned late in the season.

Rich Beck's military experience was less dramatic but had a far more dire affect on his baseball career than D-Day had on Yogi's. Rich grew up in Pasco, Washington, where he was scouted as a pitcher while in high school. His parents ran a mom-and-pop grocery store. His dad had a college scholarship that he was not able to take because he had to go to work in the store to help the family finances. So naturally he was very insistent that his son attend college, no matter how well Rich threw a baseball. So off he went, first to Columbia Basin Junior College and then to Gonzaga University in Spokane.

"I finished my college eligibility and was signed for the Yankees by Eddie Taylor," Rich recalls. "Eddie signed a lot of guys in the Northwest, like Roger Repoz and Mel Stottlemyre. The first thing he did was knock a year off my age. So all my baseball information has me listed as being born in 1941. It was really 1940. He said they might not be as interested in a guy a year older. I just went along with it. Why not?"

Rich started out not far from home, in the Class-C Pioneer League, playing at Idaho Falls. His first start was encouraging, to say the least. He pitched a no-hitter against Boise! Rich says, "It was the first no-hitter I'd had since Little League, when I shared one with my cousin. I pitched one inning, and he caught. Then we switched positions after each inning. We were sponsored by my uncle's billiard parlor." He finished 9–6 for a bad team. The

Yankees correctly concluded that he had overpowered the Pioneer League. During the winter they boosted him all the way to their Triple A roster, Richmond.

A pitcher who jumped from Class C to Triple A attracted the attention of the Phillies, who drafted Rich for the 1963 season. This meant he was technically on the big-league roster, no matter where he ended up playing during the season. He started at Chattanooga during the last year of the Class A Sally League. He lost his first two games and was sent to Bakersfield, California, in Class B. He promptly got pneumonia. It was a lost year.

1964 saw him back in Chattanooga, which was now in the Southern League. He started 5–0 but ended 5–9. Worse than his record were the uniforms of the Kansas City minor leaguers. "The A's farm team in Birmingham had to wear Charley Finley's awful uniforms," Rich remembers with loathing. "I forget all the colors they were: green, orange, blue. Really bright, like softball uniforms. A few years later the A's had those bright uniforms, too."

For 1965 the Phillies removed Beck from their major-league roster, sent him to spring training with their Triple A club, then sold him back to the Yankees two days before the season began.

"I went to Columbus, Georgia, where Loren Babe was manager, who I had back in Idaho Falls. He was a fine manager and helped everyone," Rich says. "That's where I met Roy and Bobby. I pitched 12 scoreless innings over a few relief outings to earn a starting shot. I finished 13–7, including a seven-inning no-hitter against Asheville, which was then a Pirates club. We won the pennant on the last day of the season. I pitched a two-hit shutout."

Rich attributes his success to a venerable baseball cliché come true. "I became more of a pitcher and less of a thrower," he says. "I always had a good fastball, but I learned to throw my slider, not to try and strike guys out, but to get them to hit the ball. The slider broke late just a couple of inches, so guys would swing, miss the sweet part of the bat as the ball broke, and hit little grounders to second. Bobby Murcer was my roommate. It was a fun year."

Winning the pennant earned Rich, Bobby, and I a September cup of coffee in the Bronx. In his first big-league appearance, Rich went seven innings to beat Washington 3–1. Bobby hit his first major-league homer to win it. In his next start, Rich shut out the Tigers. He walked five but didn't strike out a single batter, an unusual way to throw a shutout and certainly not easy. Cleveland beat him the last week of the season, but 2–1 with a 2.14 earned-run average looked like a rookie record with, as the baseball card said, lots of potential.

The Yankees wanted Rich to play winter ball and work on a curve, a third, bigger-breaking pitch that might give him more strikeouts and make him a dominant starter. He had just committed to a winter in Sarasota when he got his draft notice. The Yankees thought he was 25, thanks to Eddie Taylor, but he was 26, almost past the age of being drafted. However, at that stage of the Vietnam conflict, it was the older guys who were being drafted, not the 18-year-olds. Rich was at the most vulnerable age, and they got him. If he had had children, he would have been exempt. Rich was married, but his children came later.

The Yankees had a "safe spot" in the Fort Lauderdale army reserves, which they tried to get for Rich, in the manner that such spots were reserved for the privileged back then, but a brand-new law thwarted their attempt. It said that once you got your induction notice, you couldn't join the reserves. He could have gone to Canada, but he couldn't play much baseball up there, and, at the time, no one knew how long the draft would last or what would be the fate of those who returned.

Rich went to Fort Ord, California, for his initial assignment and then to Fort Hood for basic training, in Texas between Austin and Waco. "You hear a lot of stories about guys in the army getting assigned to jobs that they have no earthly qualification for," Rich says. "But not me. I had a degree in finance, and I spent my whole active duty at Fort Hood as a payroll specialist." He got out early, in November of 1967, having missed two full baseball seasons sitting behind a desk. Not much chance to work on that curveball.

Lucky for me, I found a place in the reserves before I got my induction notice. I never missed a season, but I missed a lot of weekends, especially in 1969, going to meetings. Sometimes it got pretty tiring. I remember one time we flew to Los Angeles, and I had to fly right back to New Jersey for a reserve meeting, then fly to Oakland. I don't remember how well I did on the field for those games. It felt like I was still flying around.

Not too many ballplayers served overseas in Vietnam. Al Bumbry of the Orioles is one. But a lot of us did reserve time. The Mets' Bud Harrelson sometimes went to reserve meetings with me.

Rich picked up his pitching career where it left off, going to winter ball, this time in Ponce, Puerto Rico, where Luis Arroyo, the former screwballing reliever who became famous finishing games for Whitey Ford in 1961, was manager. More significant for Rich during the off-season was the birth of his first child, Katie, a leap-year baby born on February 29, 1968, about three years late, as far as his draft board was concerned.

Rich spent the 1968 season in the Yankees' Triple A team, which was now in Syracuse. He was 5–5 with an earned-run average of 4.50, not too bad in today's offense-dominated game but pretty bad in what throughout baseball was known as "the year of the pitcher," before the mound was lowered and the strike zone shrank like a cheap cotton shirt.

He was back in Syracuse for the 1969 season, where he started badly and got worse. His location was terrible, with a lot of walks. He never got himself back on track. Frank Verdi was manager, and the team eventually won the playoffs, but Rich was gone long before that. "Verdi told me he could release me, or there was a place for me on the Mexico City team, which was the equivalent of Triple A," Rich says. "But I was married with children by then, and I didn't want to take my family all the way down to Mexico. Clyde McCullough was the manager of the Tidewater Tides, the Mets' Triple A farm club. They were in Syracuse for the game that night. I went over to Clyde and told him I was being released and asked him if they had a place for me."

Clyde suggested Rich throw for him before the game, and he'd see what he could do. "So here I was, warming up in a Syracuse uniform, throwing to the Tidewater catcher," Rich says with a chuckle. "My teammates didn't know what in the hell was going on." Clyde found a roster place for Rich at only a slight cut in pay. He lasted the year, but barely.

"I helped Tidewater a little, maybe," Rich remembers. "Won a few, lost a few." But he was nobody's idea of a prospect anymore. Of even greater importance, Rich lost a key component to being a professional baseball player. He says, "I didn't want to move anymore. Including spring training, I had moved about 40 times in six years. I probably could have caught on somewhere, hoped to develop another pitch or something. But when I was a kid I remember seeing some guys in their mid-thirties, hanging on in the low minors. I decided right then I never wanted to become like that. For the next 10 years I wondered if I quit too soon, if I had something more. But really, I think I did the right thing."

Rich worked for several years in marketing and then got his teaching certificate back in his hometown of Pasco. Sometimes his middle school and high school students discover his baseball background and ask why it never developed. "Weren't you mad when you were drafted?" they ask.

"Sure I was mad. When I got my draft notice, I balled it up and threw it across the room," he tells the kids. "But now I know I only lost a few years of baseball. A lot of guys lost a whole lot more."

Roy Gleason was one of those guys. A $100,000 bonus brought Roy to the Los Angeles Dodgers' farm system in 1961. Barely 20 years old, he entered the major-league record book late in the 1963 season, mostly as a pinch-runner for Moose Skowron. He did get one at-bat, making the best of it with a double off Dennis Bennett. As a member of the championship team that year, Roy's cup of coffee qualified him for a World Series ring.

The Dodgers were loaded then, and Gleason was still pretty raw. He spent the next few years in the minors, until he got his draft notice just before the 1967 season began. This was confusing, as Roy was the sole support of his mother and sisters, which usually was good for a deferment. The Dodgers suggested he appeal, which he did, right down to the moment he was shipped to Vietnam. He has yet to understand why his draft status was changed.

On July 24, 1968, he caught a load of shrapnel in his leg. The guy next to him was killed. He was shipped back to the States with only a shaving kit in his possession. Who knows what happened to his World Series ring?

He tried a comeback the following year, but he did not succeed. Following an early end to his dream of major-league stardom, he returned to civilian life with only might-have-beens as memories. Those, and one double.

In September 2003, however, the Dodgers proved that they, too, remembered. After throwing out the first pitch, Roy received a duplicate of his 1963 World Series ring from Dodgers manager Jim Tracy.

Chuck Goggin could relate to Roy's experience. He began in the Dodgers organization in 1964, then served 13 months with the marines in Vietnam. He stepped on a land mine in April 1967. He received a bronze star and several other citations.

He fought to get to the majors just as hard as he had as a marine. He succeeded from 1972 through 1974, when he appeared in 72 games as a utility player with the Pirates, Braves, and Red Sox, hitting .293. Who knows what his career might have been?

Wars don't affect the lives of only one generation, of course. Pitcher Danny Graves was born in Saigon in 1973, the son of a U.S. serviceman and a Vietnamese mother. He is the only player born in Vietnam in the history of the major leagues.

In 2007 Rich Beck and his wife made a trip he had not made for more than 40 years. He traveled to New York City and visited Yankee Stadium, taking the tour like any other visitor. "The clubhouse is a lot nicer now. And the seats on the bench are padded! That's new to me," Rich says. "After the game some of the players were heading through the crowd to get to their cars. I spotted Bobby Murcer." Rich's old roommate had survived a scary bout with a malignant brain tumor less than a year before. "Bobby had his head down, moving through the crowd, you know, like celebrities do. When he got close to me, I said, 'Hey, Bobby, it's Rich Beck.' Bobby's head turned up, and a big smile came across his face."

Rich Beck didn't get the career his potential indicated was possible. He was caught up in his times, like everyone. Making his old roomie smile reminded him not just of what he lost, but also what his times had given him.

chapter 5
Cups of Coffee

Roy White (left) and Horace Clarke cross bats in the Yankees locker room. Horace was a much better player than he is often given credit for being. Photo courtesy of Roy White.

Moses Leads Me Out of the Wilderness

Hitting a baseball is supposed to be the hardest thing in sports, but it came easily to me, at least as a kid back in Compton. The neighborhood guys back then played what we called "sock ball." We would tie an old sock or two really tight and use that as a ball. We couldn't afford a lot of real baseballs, but even if we could, the streets and backyards where we lived were too narrow to use them. The sock ball had the virtue of enabling us to swing away without constantly losing balls or breaking windows.

We all hit more sock-ball home runs than Mickey Mantle and Willie Mays, but that didn't mean it was easy. You could throw some very nasty curves with it, and I believe seeing so many breaking sock balls helped me later on.

I could always hit, and, for my size—5'10", 170 pounds—I hit with power. I did so well my first spring training in 1962 that I was sent to Greensboro in what was then Class B, a much higher classification than a rookie usually saw. I lasted only 25 games there and hit just over .200. It was a lot to get used to, playing professional baseball. No sock balls to hit. What made it even harder was that the old ballfield in Greensboro looked like a strong wind would blow it over, and the lights were bad enough that you could get mugged in the outfield and not be able to recognize the thief.

I was relieved to be sent "down" to Fort Lauderdale, which had a brand-new ballpark and, even better, brand-new lights. I started stinging the ball, but it kept being caught. It seemed like every night I was being robbed. This wasn't just my opinion.

"It got so we wouldn't sit next to him in the dugout," Ian Dixon, my old friend and Florida State League teammate remembers. "We wouldn't shake his hand. We were afraid it would rub off, that we would catch his bad luck."

I knew I was better than I was showing, and I just kept swinging. I ended up at .286, so the hits did start to fall. Like a lot of lower classifications, this was a pitcher's league, and .286 came close to leading the league. I hit three homers, and Dixon's five led the league.

The next year I was in Columbus, Georgia, in the Southern League, fast company. I got off to a great start, but then I got just about the worst injury I ever had in baseball. I was trying to beat out a ground ball and at the last minute had to avoid a collision with first baseman Lee May. Lee might not have been as huge as he was later with Cincinnati, but he was still at least 195 pounds and solid as a rock.

My left eye tried to occupy the same space as Lee's elbow and lost. I was a mess. But I could have recovered from a black eye. The bad part was that the blow affected the nerves in my jaw, and I couldn't open my mouth to eat, except for soup and oatmeal. You can't hit .300 on soup and oatmeal. I missed several games, and, when I came back, I was weak and my timing was off. My final stats weren't that great, and I was back in Columbia the next year.

In 1965 I hit .300 with 19 homers and was the Southern League MVP. By September 7, 1965, I was in Yankee Stadium. In my mind I was way ahead of schedule. When I signed with the Yankees right out of high school, instead of taking a baseball scholarship to UCLA, I gave myself five or six years to make the majors, and here I was in fewer than four.

In my first game, manager Johnny Keane sent me to pinch-hit for Al Downing. I hit a 3–2 fastball off Dave McNally up the middle for a single. It was a doubleheader, and I started the second game at second base, hit leadoff, and got two hits off Wally Bunker, including my first double. For the rest of the year, I hit .333 in 42 at-bats. The next 14 years would not be that easy, but I had gotten my chance and wasn't about to blow it. A big reason I was there ahead of schedule and was able to keep hitting was a coach named Wally Moses.

Wally was a Yankees hitting coach, instructor, and scout during my minor- and early major-league years. He later moved to Detroit, where he was a coach of the championship Tigers of 1968. We were about the same size, we both played outfield, and, if you look at both of our lifetime batting records, you will see a similarity: we were all-around hitters—some power, speed, and walks. We also shared a funny irony about our names. I'm not White, and Moses wasn't Jewish.

In the early 1930s, after Hank Greenberg made it big as a Jewish baseball star in Detroit, the New York teams began to beat the bushes for Jewish players. Moses, a native of Georgia, was tearing up all the minor leagues in the South, when a scout for the New York Giants discovered him. Sadly, Wally had to explain that he was not of the desired faith. The scout, apparently forgetting that Moses was a fine hitter regardless of his religion, did not sign him. I assume that many players were denied chances because of anti-Semitism. Moses must be the only player not to get signed because of pro-Semitism.

Fortunately, Connie Mack of the Philadelphia A's was an equal-opportunity employer, as long as you worked cheap. He was in the process of discarding the expensive stars that had given him championships in the early 1930s and was looking for young fellows like Moses, who could play and be happy for the chance. So Wally began, in 1935, a 17-year career of good hitting for bad teams. His only World Series appearance was in 1946 with the Red Sox. At age 35 he had been picked up for late-season pennant insurance and got five hits as the Sox right fielder in a losing cause.

He was only in his early fifties when he was helping me, but with his white hair and the wrinkles earned by players who per-formed mostly during the day, to me he looked as old as, well, Moses.

You didn't get a lot of coaching back in those days, and what you got was as likely to hurt you as help you. One player might have been able to use what a coach was teaching, while another would not.

For instance, Mike Hegan was a bonus boy with the Yankees who came through their system the same years as I did. We were often teammates, and he remains a friend today as he continues his long post-playing career as a broadcaster with Cleveland. He was 6'1", 190 pounds and, in the words of the day, "looked like a ballplayer." He also had good bloodlines. His father, Jim, was a fine catcher for the Indians who played on pennant-winners in 1948 and 1954, catching one of the most outstanding pitching staffs of all time.

Perhaps he inherited his father's talents too precisely. That is, he was a gifted defensive player who couldn't hit. This was tolerated in his father because he was a catcher, but Mike played first base. Wally was assigned the task of teaching Mike to pull the ball so he could hit with the power necessary for a big-league first baseman. Wally tried very hard. So did Mike. But the results just weren't there. Maybe it was because Wally wasn't a pull-hitter. Maybe they should have gotten somebody like Ted Williams to work with Mike.

Maybe Moses needed a miracle.

One time, Mike got so frustrated he told Wally to, well, attempt a sexual act upon himself. This was in the early 1960s before "f-bombs" were thrown around so casually everywhere, especially toward authority figures. Wally did not perform the act on himself, and Mike did not learn to pull the ball. Mike's glove kept him in the majors for 12 years, but he averaged only about four homers per year.

I never forgot the advice Wally gave me, because it helped me so many times in my career. Every major-league player has one or more special talents he falls back on when he needs it. For me it was a quick bat. I could wait a long time before swinging. This enabled me to read whether the pitch was a fastball, curveball, slider, or whatever. Every split second counts at bat, and my ability to wait got and kept me in the major leagues.

What few of us understand, whether we are athletes or not, is that one's strength can become one's weakness. This happened to me when I began to wait *too* long before swinging. I was quick, but I wasn't Superman. If I waited too long, I would pull away from the ball, come out of my crouch, and start hitting annoying little grounders. The next thing you know, you're destroying watercoolers.

When I would get in a slump, it was almost always because of this. It wasn't exactly like Luke Skywalker hearing Obi-Wan Kenobi telling him to "Use the Force, Luke," but I always remembered

Wally telling me, "Slow everything down. Get that bat started. Don't wait so long, and you'll be fine." And I always was.

The Phantom Double-Play Combination

We were billed as "the Yankee Double-Play Combination of the Future." Bobby Murcer at short and Roy White at second. Bobby became a great friend of mine almost immediately, and I lost a great friend when he died of a brain tumor in the summer of 2008. Of course, it wasn't just me that lost. All of baseball did. The great talent Bobby had on the field was matched, maybe even exceeded, by his ability to be friendly and loyal to so many people. This trait came across as a broadcaster. I'm here to tell you, it was real. I'm glad Bobby was able to share some of his memories here.

The Yankees I signed with in 1961 were a legendary team. They continued winning through 1964, but, wouldn't you know it, just as I joined them at the end of 1965, they headed downhill. The core was gone, either traded, retired, or on the downside of their careers. Mickey Mantle and Whitey Ford were fighting through lingering, difficult injuries. My first years in the majors have been tagged "the Horace Clarke Era" of Yankees history, with a measure of derision.

It wasn't necessarily a bad time for everybody. As Bobby Murcer remembered, "The Horace Clarke Era was good for Roy and me. It gave us opportunities that we wouldn't have had a few years before." Any number of Yankees farmhands found themselves traded or languishing in the minors waiting for Tony Kubek and Bobby Richardson to retire. In a way, though, we discovered there can be such a thing as too much opportunity.

Although it took me a few years to reach the majors, Bobby's first at-bat, at the end of 1965, came when he was barely 19. Perhaps because he was from Oklahoma and was perceived as a power-hitting shortstop, he was billed as "the Next Mickey Mantle."

"There was never any particular moment when I knew I belonged in the majors, because when I signed a contract, I signed to play with the Yankees," Bobby remembered. "I never doubted myself. I never thought about it any other way than that I would be a Yankee. I was pretty naïve back then." What 18-year-old isn't, especially one being told he is to replace a legend? "Maybe that naïveté helped me," Murcer concluded, "protect[ed] me from having any doubts."

There was only one problem with the Yankee Double-Play Combination of the Future, featuring the Next Mickey Mantle. We never played together. At the end of 1965, I got into a few games, in both the outfield and at second, but never with Bobby at short. He got into 11 games there but made five errors.

"I was unseasoned. I didn't know the little things about playing short. Just having a strong arm isn't enough," Bobby explained. "I had the arm and range, but you need to throw off balance, be an acrobat, throw accurately without being able to plant your feet." Patrons sitting behind first base could attest to Bobby's strong arm but not to its accuracy. There could have been a good business created by an insurance salesman, selling policies to box-seat patrons when Bobby was an infielder.

By the time I got to the big leagues, management was already nearly committed to my being an outfielder, not that they ever told me. I played only three major-league games at second. Like Bobby, I had the range and arm strength but not the quickness to make the short, quick throws or the double play. I was made for left field, as everyone finally discovered, though I played all the out-field positions, even a little third base, and took several years to settle. Horace Clarke, meanwhile, settled in at second.

Horace was a little second baseman from the Virgin Islands, who played regularly from 1967 to 1973. He couldn't hit with any-thing close to my power, but he was quick and agile. Contrary to uninformed popular opinion, Horace was a good ballplayer, a hustler who wanted to play every day. You can look it up. His hitting was a bit under average, but his fielding was way above. His only crime was not being Bobby Richardson, though if Bobby had played during those years, it's not likely he could have won pennants by himself.

Horace had a great attitude about all this. He'd just say, "I don't care. Whatever happens, I'm going back to the islands and fish." And that's just what he did, a good deal richer than when he first left home.

The opportunity that the Horace Clarke Era gave players like me, Bobby, Roger Repoz, Jake Gibbs, Mike Hegan, and others was not always an advantage. We were all rushed to the majors without the experience necessary to master the tasks we were given. Bobby and I eventually prevailed, but not everybody did.

Meanwhile, the Murcer-as-shortstop experiment lasted a little longer. "When I got there in 1966, Richardson was still at second, and Ruben Amaro, an excellent fielder but a light hitter, was supposed to platoon with me," Bobby said. "But Ruben got hurt about the fifth game of the season, out for the year. They moved Cletis Boyer from third to shortstop, and Tom Tresh went to third from the outfield. Tommy was a great athlete. He could play anywhere. Eventually, Horace Clarke played a lot of shortstop that year, also, before finding his home on the other side of the diamond. And Bobby Murcer went…where?"

To Toledo. After seven games in New York, Bobby was on pace to make about 50 errors. Thus, he became the Mud Hen shortstop, going down in the history of that storied minor-league franchise as its scariest shortstop ever. The Bobby Murcer infield experiment was over. Shortly thereafter, the Yankees discovered that Roy White and Bobby Murcer were not the double-play combination of their future but two-thirds of a pretty good outfield.

What a Difference Four Years Makes

Two of the young men who came out of Morris High School in the Bronx, both born in 1937, hold enviable accomplishments. One man had been on the Morris High track team. His name was Colin Powell, and he became secretary of state. The other man was on the baseball team. That was Art Lopez, and he played 38 games for the New York Yankees. Ask most American males, and you will find more envy for Lopez than Powell.

Neither started out aiming for what they attained. Powell was a geology major at City College in New York. Ironically, Art Lopez was in the military before Powell. "I went into the navy right out of high school. Technically, I'm a Korean War vet, because the war was still going on when I enlisted. I played baseball in high school and did well, but for some reason I didn't think about going further." There were not a lot of Puerto Rican players in the major leagues then.

Ruben Gomez started pitching for the Giants in 1953. Vic Power played mostly outfield and only in a few games at first for the Philadelphia A's in 1954. These were the only two Puerto Ricans in the majors for anything more than a brief trial during Art's prime baseball rooting years, before he joined the navy.

Power might have arrived in Yankee Stadium a few years earlier, but he was not considered the "right kind" of player to be the first black Yankee. A native of the colorblind Puerto Rican culture, Vic never played by the rules of American segregation well enough to impress the Yankees front office of the 1950s. It wasn't until Art was already in the navy that Roberto Clemente and then Orlando Cepeda became Puerto Rican superstars.

When Art got out of the navy he was already married. He worked in a bank and was considering banking as a career. He played baseball only once a week, on the sandlots of the Bronx, near his old high school. It was also not far from Yankee Stadium. "For the Yankees, I was a neighborhood guy," Art says. "I used to run around a track during gym class where the new stadium is going to be. After the navy, I was playing well on the weekends, enjoying myself, so I went to a tryout at Yankee Stadium. I was 5'9", 160 pounds, and I could run."

The scouts said, "If you gain 12 pounds, we will sign you."

"I was back there as soon as I could be," Art says, "weighing 172."

So now the Yankees had a very fast outfielder that could hit, was 5'9", and weighed 172 pounds. But they did not know about another number associated with Art Lopez. He was 24 years old. They knew he was out of high school. They just didn't know how *far* out.

"They might not have signed me if they knew I was 24. I was a young, fast, good-looking kid, and I looked younger than I was." Art did not go out of his way to correct what might have been a Yankees misapprehension. He just started hitting.

"I went to a rookie league and hit about 10 homers in 30 games," Art remembers. He hit like a man among boys because, even at 5'9", he was. Most of the competition would have been just out of high school or college. He was soon advanced to Auburn, of the New York–Pennsylvania League, where he continued to excel. Now he was no longer taking advantage of callow youth; he was still hitting everything they threw.

He continued to advance, fighting prejudice against his size every step of the way. The fact that he wasn't going to hit many balls over the fence hurt him, too, especially with the Yankees, who judged all their outfielders as if they were looking for the next Mantle, the next DiMaggio. It was hard for an Art Lopez, or, just a bit later and just a bit bigger, a Roy White to be taken seriously by Yankees brass. The smaller outfielder had to do more to impress.

"I was at a disadvantage because I just hit lefty. Mantle made the Yankees eager to find other switch-hitters," Art remembers. "They found another good one in Tom Tresh, then along came Roy and also Horace Clarke. I never hit lefties as well as righties. Few lefty hitters do. And while I was fast in the outfield, I had a sore arm almost my whole career, so I didn't throw as well as they wanted."

Still, Art progressed and was appreciated enough to win the award for the outstanding rookie in the Yankees' spring training camp in 1965. Among his competitors were a second baseman named Roy White and a shortstop named Bobby Murcer.

Art made the team for opening day but started only five games and was sent down to Triple A in midseason. He returned in September. Bobby and I were called up then, too. For us, 1965 was our first major-league experience. For Art Lopez, it was his first and last. Part of the reason may be that the infielders Murcer and White were now the outfielders Murcer and White, more competition for Art. "They moved Roy to the outfield to take advantage of his speed," Art says. But competition wasn't the whole reason.

"The Yankees found out I was 28, not 24," Art says. "Suddenly I wasn't much of a prospect in their eyes." Art suggests that he knows the player who spilled the beans on him, but don't ask him who it is. Unlike this teammate, Art isn't talking.

He bounced around the Yankees' minor-league system, now an "aging veteran," always hitting well but going nowhere. The Yankees suggested he might find some success in Japan and paved the way east for him. In Japan, Art didn't seem so small, and his arm, due to the shorter fences, didn't seem so sore. He prospered there from 1968 through 1974.

"I made much more money there than I ever did, or would have, playing in the States," Art says. His roommate in Japan was George Altman, who had a few pretty good years in the National League, then became one of the first American stars in Japan. He credited martial arts with keeping him in shape, something I found helpful, too.

Altman may also be the only player in history to play both in Japan and the old Negro Leagues. George played a year for the old Kansas City Monarchs not long before that famous franchise folded.

"By the time I was ready to throw in the towel, the Japanese wanted me to recommend another player," Art says. "I thought of Roy. He still had a few years left in the majors then, but I knew he might have something left, even when he retired from the big leagues. He was always in shape and took care of himself." Art showed me the way to three years in Japan after I left the Yankees. A minor claim to fame resulted, in that I am the only player to hit in front of both Mickey Mantle and Sadaharu Oh.

During the years that Art was trying to make the Yankees and have the opportunity to play big-league baseball in his own neighborhood, the team was sold to CBS. A lot of things changed on the team then, in addition to the passing of the old Mantle-Ford-Berra Yankees to a younger group, including myself, who, at the time, were a little too green to carry on the winning tradition just yet. It was the new Yankees manager, Johnny Keane, who picked Art as Yankee Rookie of the Year during spring training. The Yankees had one of their worst years in 1965, and Keane, who managed us only that one year and the beginning of the next, got a lot of blame. Even Yankees historians often consider Keane at best an ill fit for the team. Art has a simpler answer.

"A player has a good year, he loves the manager. He has a bad year, he hates the manager," Art concludes. He still cherishes his brief Yankees career. "I was just thrilled to be there. Me, a Puerto Rican Yankee!"

Over the years, the two Morris High graduates faced some tough assignments. Colin Powell had to command troops in the first Gulf War; he was secretary of state for the second. Yet he might have gotten off easily compared to his old schoolmate, Art Lopez. Art teaches elementary school in Washington, D.C. In 2007, at the age of 70, he earned his master's degree.

Art Lopez is no longer fast or young, but by all accounts he is still 5'9" and good-looking.

chapter 6
Batting Cleanup

Mickey Mantle blasts his 500th home run into the stands on May 14, 1967.

Homer Mania

I hit .333 in a late-season call-up in 1965 and was feeling pretty good about myself. If I had gone to college I would just now be graduating, and I was already in the big leagues. The Yankees were a team in transition. They had lost more games than they won for the first time in 40 years. There were opportunities for young players that had not existed in decades. I was ready.

A week into the 1966 season, I started in center field and hit my first major-league home run off Sam McDowell, who threw as hard as anyone ever has. A week later, I went deep against the Red Sox's Earl Wilson. I was hitting .375, with a slugging percentage of .667. I thought I might be the new Willie Mays, and, as the home-run-hitting center fielder of the New York Yankees, I thought, "This isn't so hard."

Wrong.

Even Reggie Jackson has said it is almost impossible to hit a home run when you are trying to hit home runs. I found that out the hard way. Three weeks later, I was down to .280 and had not yet hit my third home run. In June I fell to .225, which is where I finished. I played myself out of the starting lineup. I finished with seven homers, a few less than might be expected of the new Willie Mays.

The worst part about hitting a few homers is that your body wants to keep hitting them even after your mind has wised up. That is, back in the 1960s, unless you were Mickey Mantle, Frank Howard, Moose Skowron, or a very few others, hitting homers required pulling the ball, getting your bat out in front of the plate really quickly, jerking your hips open. If you've been going for the long ball for a few weeks and then decide that line drives are the better part of valor, it takes a while for your body to get the message. It still wants to go long. The result is that you pull off the ball and give pitchers and infielders nice gifts: pop-up after pop-up after pop-up.

First I lost my starting job, and, in spring training the next year, I even lost my seat on a big-league bench.

In 1967 the Yankees loaned me to the Dodgers' Triple A farm club in Spokane, Washington. The idea was that I would fill a spot on that club, then be returned to the Yankees if and when they wanted me back. Still, there were persistent rumors that the Dodgers liked me and would work out a deal for me. At the time, it was uncertain whether my future would be in the infield or outfield, but I was a "Dodgers-type" player: fast, could steal bases, some power, switch-hitter. Going back to the years of Maury Wills and Jim Gilliam, the Dodgers always seemed to like switch-hitters that could run and make contact at the top of their batting orders.

I was hitting .343 in mid-July and might have led the Pacific Coast League in hitting, when the Yankees wanted me back. Dick Howser had broken his arm, and they needed another versatile guy off the bench. I tried to impress everyone a little too much. I was filling in at various positions and couldn't get anything going. I finished at .224 with only two homers. The numbers don't lie. I realized once and for all that I was not a home-run hitter.

I started choking up to remind myself that I wasn't going for homers. I used a short swing and hit to all fields. When I got two strikes, I choked up a couple of inches more. I pinch-hit for the first week of the 1968 season and, wouldn't you know it, now that I knew I wasn't a home-run hitter, I hit one out in my first start, against the Angels' Jim McGlothlin. I was a regular somewhere in the outfield for the rest of the year and the rest of my career.

I hit 17 homers in 1968, my first year as a non–home run hitter, and I got 160 during my career. I had enough power to hit cleanup in 387 games and enough speed to hit leadoff in 192, though I more often hit second or third.

I hit .267 in 1968, which is a bit below my lifetime average, but it was the Year of the Pitcher, and there weren't more than a dozen or so hitters who had higher averages.

A lot of players still think they might be the new Willie Mays, and for a week or a month, they might be. Then reality comes to call. Fortunately, being the first Roy White worked out well for me.

The Breaks of the Game

In 1966 a number of young players were trying to find a place on the Yankees. Some, like Bobby Murcer and me, were lucky enough to stay a long time. Others, like Steve Whitaker or Mike Ferraro, never got established in the big leagues. Jake Gibbs did both. He played all or part of 10 years, yet he never had the career his athleticism promised.

Broken fingers on his throwing hand, an occupational hazard of catching, hurt Jake's development in both 1963 and 1964. In August 1966 Jake had already appeared in 62 games as a backup for Elston Howard, who was 37 and in his last year as the regular catcher. Jake was hitting .258, which doesn't seem like much today, but the league average that year, dominated by pitchers throwing off the old 15" mound, was only .240.

I was sitting on the bench, and Jake was catching Al Downing in the stadium against Detroit's Earl Wilson. If you don't remember Earl Wilson, think of a right-handed Dontrelle Willis. Earl was a big guy who, like Willis and Downing, were among the very few African American pitchers to have 20-win seasons. Plus, both Willis and Wilson were dangerous hitters, in more ways than one.

Wilson hit 35 homers in his career, one fewer than Wes Ferrell, the all-time leader. He was also dangerous because he had a huge swing, which often turned his whole body around. You didn't want to be in the way of Earl Wilson when he was at bat.

His first attempt that day, he popped out harmlessly to Gibbs in foul territory. In his second, Wilson screwed himself into the ground, swung, and there was a pop like a rifle shot. It sounded like someone had doubled into the outfield gap, but Wilson didn't make contact. With the ball, that is. What he made contact with was Jake Gibbs' left arm. Wilson's backswing was so vicious he broke the smaller bone in Gibbs' left forearm. What sounded like an extra-base hit was the sound of Jake Gibbs' season ending. Howard replaced him behind the plate. In Wilson's fourth at-bat he homered off Hal Reniff. Mantle won the game with what we now call a walk-off two-run homer against Hank Aguirre.

One of the reasons Jake Gibbs chose baseball was because he thought it would be safer than football. It wasn't for Jake Gibbs.

Jake is one of two Yankees to be inducted in the College Football Hall of Fame, for his three outstanding years quarterbacking at the University of Mississippi. The other Yankees football great was Jackie Jensen, who is remembered primarily as a member of the Boston Red Sox and Most Valuable Player in the league in 1958.

In 1948 Jackie was a running back for the University of California, leading them to the Rose Bowl victory in a season where he rushed for more than 1,000 and averaged more than seven yards per carry. The year before, he led the University of California baseball team to its first national championship. Along the way he outpitched a University of Texas hurler named Bobby Layne, later of NFL glory, and also played against a light-hitting Yale first baseman named George Bush. By 1950, he was in the Yankees outfield and the World Series.

But the Yankees had another kid, one who never played football beyond his little Oklahoma high school. Mickey Mantle took over center field, and the gifted Jensen found himself a Washington Senator. He had some decent years but didn't blossom until he moved from Griffith Stadium's cavernous left field to Fenway Park's inviting Green Monster. Several years of 20 homers and more than 100 RBIs followed.

There was every reason to think that Jake Gibbs, choosing baseball over football, would find success as Jensen had. But after that injury, though he caught more games than any other Yankee during the next three years, he never hit like he did in 1966. When a rookie named Thurman Munson came along, Gibbs was a reserve catcher once more.

In 1970 he hit .301 with eight homers in only 153 at-bats. He came back for 1971, announcing that, at age 32, it would be his last year. Since 1965 he had gone back to Ole Miss and coached the quarterbacks every fall. He was tired of being away from home for half the year, especially when it looked like he had more future coaching in Mississippi than he did playing in New York.

Then one day, when the Senators were in town, Gibbs was around the batting cage when he heard an unmistakable voice. It had the volume, cadence, and swagger of John Wayne in *True Grit*. "What the hell are you quitting for?" Ted Williams asked, or rather bellowed. "We tried to trade for you twice! Your damn team must think a lot of you, because we sure as hell couldn't get you!"

"After I announced I was retiring, Williams tried to get me for one of their prime prospects, Mike Epstein," Gibbs says. "It made me feel good that Williams thought I could play for him, but I had already decided I was leaving."

Gibbs ended up coaching the University of Mississippi baseball team from 1971 to 1990. He won the Southeast Conference title in his first year.

"Over the years I coached Pete Ladd, Steve Dillard, Tucker Ashford," Jake says. "Tucker was a quarterback, too. I had Jeff Fassero for one year. We only recruited back then within a 300-mile radius, but we had some pretty good teams. Each of the players I had reach the majors was outstanding in college, but you really can't tell who will make the majors, unless it is somebody like Will Clark or Rafael Palmiero. Anyone could see their talent. I can't tell you how many great arms never make it to the big leagues."

Jake never regretted his decision and cherishes his Yankees years and teammates. However, he muses, "It's funny how things go. I quit partly to be closer to home. If Williams had traded for me the next year, 1972, the Senators moved to Texas. I might have been a Texas Ranger, closer to home and still playing baseball."

Jake Gibbs knows the breaks of the game.

Tape Measure

In some ways Mickey Mantle was a shadow of his former self by the time I joined the team, but he was still Mickey Mantle, at least sometimes. I remember the first astounding Mantle home run I

Puerto Rican youngsters plead for Mickey Mantle's autograph from their dugout-roof perch before the New York Yankees–Washington Senators exhibition game in San Juan, Puerto Rico, on April 5, 1965.

saw personally. It opened my eyes. It was July 23, 1966. Marcelino Lopez of the Angels started against us on a Saturday afternoon at the stadium. It was a big midsummer crowd. Al Downing started for us. He and Lopez were two of the hardest-throwing young lefties in baseball, and both were just wild enough to keep you loose at the plate.

Al was already behind 3–0 in the third, courtesy of the first three Angels hitting doubles and Bobby Knoop going long in the top of the second. A walk and two singles brought up Mickey with the bases loaded, one out. Lopez threw a fastball up and away to Mickey, batting right-handed. He got on top of it and tomahawked it to the farthest corner of the third deck. It was no lazy fly. It was a dangerous line drive. You could hear it bouncing around under the overhang. The grand slam gave us the lead.

Now, it was a rarity when a lefty hit one in the third deck. Usually it would be a high fly that would sort of settle into the seats. The one Mantle hit was scary. If you had asked me, I would have said a right-handed hitter couldn't do that. Nobody can hit it that far to the opposite field. He did it—and at a time when he was supposed to be finished.

This should not have surprised me. In May he also hit an opposite-field homer in Yankee Stadium, this time batting left-handed. He hit one to right field in the first inning off Dean Chance. But it was the next one that got my attention. Lew Burdette was 39 years old, mopping up for the Angels after star-ring for many years with the Milwaukee Braves. He beat the Yankees three times in the 1957 World Series. He didn't even throw hard then, depending on a variety of curves, sliders, and a sinker that he never even pretended wasn't a spitter. Now he was that walking cliché of the pitcher who didn't throw hard enough to break a pane of glass.

Lew dropped some little dinky curve over the outside corner, low and away. Mickey hit where it was pitched, to left. If you have ever seen World Series highlights from 1947, you will remember Al Gionfriddo's leaping catch against the fence in Death Valley, the deepest part of left center, where the sign on the fence said

402. Joe DiMaggio, the batter Al robbed, is seen kicking the dirt near second base. It's remembered as much for Joe's rare show of onfield emotion as for the great catch. Well, Mickey hit that slow curve about 30 or 40 feet beyond the *402* sign, even though the pitch was so slow he had to provide every bit of energy. It didn't seem possible that anyone could hit a ball that hard to the opposite field. Mantle could, from either side. I don't know if any other batter in baseball history could. I thought to myself, *Now I've seen the real Mickey Mantle.*

And, lest I forget, when we were in Fenway Park in June, in consecutive games, Mickey hit two homers each, one to left and one to right. This time they all came batting lefty, first against Jose Santiago, then against our old teammate, Rollie Sheldon. Mickey was still Mickey, right to the end, just not as often. What he could do to a baseball was truly, to use the current term, *awesome.* I had always heard about "tape measure" homers. Now I had seen a few, hit by the guy who caused the term to be invented.

500 for Mickey and 10 for Dooley

Dooley Womack was responsible for making sure that my career as a catcher lasted exactly zero games. Not that I aspired to catch, or that anyone suggested it, but the minor-league situation in the 1960s required that everybody do a little bit of everything.

Today even the lowest minor-league teams seem to have almost as many coaches as players. When Dooley and I were at Columbus in the Southern League in 1964, most teams just had a manager who doubled as a third-base coach and one coach who handled first. A roving pitching coach came around about as often as the full moon. Bullpen coaches and catchers were luxuries unknown.

One day when I wasn't going to play, I went down to the bullpen. I must have had a sprained ankle or some other little injury that needed a day off. All the players had to do their parts. We warmed up pitchers. We carried the equipment bags. Part of the reason I headed for the pen that day was that Dooley was starting, and, well, I knew that he didn't throw all that hard and had good control. I figured he wouldn't be that hard for me to catch.

I also knew that he was a sinker-slider pitcher. That is, most of his pitches broke downward. I crouched down really low, determined not to let anything get by me.

Dooley let fly, and I hunkered down even lower, which would have been a good strategy had Dooley not thrown a fastball. I had to leap up to catch it. This put my face directly in the flight of the ball. Fortunately, my glove arrived an instant before the ball, saving this underpaid minor-league ballplayer a lot of money on bridgework for the teeth that supposedly not-hard-throwing Dooley Womack's fastball would have surely loosened.

My career as a bullpen catcher lasted exactly one pitch. Who would have thought it was harder to catch a pitch than hit it?

Dooley started his career back in 1958. He wandered around the bush leagues for a few years without impressing many people, but as he got a little older he got a little stronger, and his pitches began to move. He performed fairly well for the next few years and was invited to spring training with the big club more than once before he finally stuck. In 1965 he led the International League with an earned-run average of 2.17 as a Toledo Mud Hen. So in 1966 he had a great chance to make the team, but he wasn't exactly brimming with confidence. "My locker was next to the door, so it always felt to me like it would be easy to shove me out," Dooley says.

Mickey Mantle helped him relax. "The first day of spring training, he went around the locker room to all the rookies saying, 'Hi, I'm Mickey Mantle.' It really helped take the pressure off. He knew that it was kind of hard for the younger players to know how to act around him. We all put him on a pedestal." Mickey's willingness to step down from that pedestal is one of the reasons his plaque in Yankee Stadium has, as its first line, "A great teammate."

Dooley made the final cut out of spring training and flew north with the team. We flew to Atlanta for a final exhibition game. "We were sitting on the runway ready to fly to New York, when the pilot comes over the intercom and says, 'I've got a light on my panel. We have to check it out.'" Dooley says. "I look out and see all these fire engines coming toward the plane, and I'm thinking, 'Oh, no!' I just made the majors, and I'm gonna die on the runway in Atlanta before I even get into a game!"

It turned out the only thing that was wrong was that a light on the pilot's panel was out, so everybody lived to see the season open. Even Dooley Womack, who still didn't quite believe. "Back then they had 30 days to pare down the roster to 25, so even making the team out of spring training didn't mean that you were up for the year. Three or four guys always were sent down after a few games."

Dooley's roommate was Jack Cullen, another pitcher, who had been up and down with the Yankees two other years, but he was still technically a rookie. For the first few weeks of the season, both Dooley and Jack got only a few innings of work. Mantle again helped by telling Womack, "If you didn't belong up here, you wouldn't be here." But Dooley still knew that somebody who was here wasn't going to stay.

In early May, Cullen gave up three runs in one inning to the Indians. That night Ralph Houk called their hotel room. Houk had returned as manager after a three-year absence. When Dooley answered the phone and found it was the manager, he gulped. But Ralph asked for Cullen and told him he had been optioned back to the minors.

A few days later, Dooley came into a game against the Twins and got Rich Rollins on a grounder with two on and two out. The next inning, he struck out Tony Oliva, Andy Kosco, and Harmon Killebrew. When he came into the dugout, Houk told him, "You've made the team."

Steve Hamilton, Pedro Ramos, and Hal Reniff were still the bullpen workhorses, but Dooley got into 42 games. He finally convinced himself he belonged when, the following year, he became the Yankees' bullpen ace, recording 18 saves in 65 games. Both totals were fourth-highest in the league.

Most memorable for Dooley about that 1967 season, however, was that he was the winning pitcher in the game when Mantle hit home run No. 500.

Then, as now, a hitter getting 500 long ones is a big event. It was even more so back then, when only four previous hitters had done it: Babe Ruth, Jimmie Foxx, Ted Williams, and Mel Ott. Mickey hit 499 on May 3 and then hit just about nothing for the next 10 games or so.

Womack relieved Mel Stottlemyre on May 14, in the sixth inning against the Orioles in New York. The O's scored four that inning to take a 4–3 lead; we came back in the bottom of the inning with two of our own. Then, in the seventh, Mickey connected off Stu Miller. It was the only extra-base hit Mantle ever got off the extremely slowballing Miller, who usually frustrated the hell out of big swingers.

Dooley remembers the scene well. He says, "Mantle ran around the bases with his head down, as usual, then stood on the front steps of the dugout, spun around, and fell into the dugout saying, 'It's over! It's over! It's finally over!'"

It was a good thing he hit it. A few innings later, Mantle gave the run back when, playing first, he threw wildly past third, allowing Frank Robinson to score. Womack was the winning pitcher, 6–5. It was the 10th win of his career. "Mantle was moved to first more because of his arm than his legs," Dooley recalls. "As many times as he hurt his legs, he could still run, but his arm was gone. I guess it did save his legs to play first, though."

Later in the year, Dooley found out personally just how fast even the aging Commerce Comet could run. "One day we were just loosening up in the outfield, and I said, 'Hey, Mickey, let's run sprints. He said, 'Yeah!' and just took off. All I saw after that was the number seven in my face," Dooley says. "He was still really fast. We ran about 10 sprints."

"If we did this every day, I bet my legs would be a lot better," Mantle said.

"But you didn't ask Mickey Mantle to run sprints every day," Dooley laments. "Nobody did. He was Mickey Mantle. He was such a regular guy, I don't think he ever realized how high all his teammates put him, especially in his last years, when all the guys he had come up with were gone."

Dooley Womack says, "Mickey Mantle was my idol. He still is."

chapter 7

It's a Long Season

Lou Piniella was always cracking jokes and had a unique chemistry with the rest of the players. He began his long managerial career with the Yankees from 1986–1988, but he never took them to the playoffs.

Managers Three

When a person is in school, you never think that some of the goof-offs you hung around with would grow up to be teachers. Then there were others who didn't surprise you at all, who acted like adults even when they were kids. It is the same with your old teammates who become managers. I've played with several.

Lou Piniella was a guy you wouldn't automatically have picked out of the clubhouse as a future manager. I go way back with Lou. I first saw him in the Carolina League. He bounced around several organizations before he landed in the big leagues with Kansas City. His ticket was punched by Cleveland, Washington, Baltimore, Cleveland again, then Seattle. When he finally got a chance to play regularly with the Royals, he was American League Rookie of the Year for 1969.

He was a character, always cracking jokes and needling other players. He was a big part of our pennant-winning chemistry, whether it was jesting on the bus or ragging on a teammate. There was a constant battle between Lou and Catfish Hunter.

"Considering the distance of that home run you gave up tonight, I should have been playing in the upper deck with a net," Lou would say to the Cat, loud enough for the whole clubhouse to hear.

"The way you catch the ball, a net might help," Hunter would shoot back. Then he would mock Piniella's voice. Lou considered himself kind of a slick Tampa gangsta, if there had been "gangstas" in the 1970s and if they were white guys who also spoke Spanish. His usual way of speaking was loudly, with a kind of nasal, Jimmy Cagney, wiseguy voice. Catfish would repeat everything Lou said, imitating his voice and how he would storm around when he lost his temper, which was frequently. So, Lou wasn't a lock to be a manager, though his ability to keep his teams loose, yet yank them when they need it, doesn't surprise me.

Bobby Cox has joined that rare fraternity, including Sparky Anderson, Tommy Lasorda, and Tony La Russa, whose major-league playing careers warranted no attention whatsoever but who reached the big leagues as managers and stayed for decades of success. Bobby began his professional career in 1959 in the Dodgers organization. He then went to the minor-league organizations of the Cubs and Braves without ever rising to the big leagues. The Yankees traded Bob Tillman and Dale Roberts for him in December 1967. When you trade away Bob Tillman and the other team has snookered you, well, that gives you an idea of Bobby's total big-league career: a .225 lifetime batting average in 220 Yankees games.

I didn't think he was that bad of a player. He had good hands, and he hit in the minors. He was in that parade of third basemen who failed to replace Cletis Boyer when he was traded in 1969, until Graig Nettles arrived from Cleveland in 1973. I never imagined Cox as a manager or thought that he would be interested.

I do remember one thing about Bobby. When we went to Anaheim, the organist sometimes played music when you came to bat. It wasn't like today when everybody has his own theme song. Good grief, if two guys choose the same song, like Mariano Rivera and Billy Wagner—New York's two dominant closers—did with Metallica's "Enter Sandman," the radio sports-talk shows act like the Entertainment Network would if Renee Zellweger and Nicole Kidman wore the same Versace to the Oscars or something.

Anyway, Bobby used to walk with his head kind of lunging forward a bit. He still does. The Anaheim organist played "Turkey in the Straw" when Cox came to bat. So, yes, after you noticed it, he did sort of walk like a turkey. Of course, once it was pointed out, with the sensitivity that has characterized ballplayers of every generation, we never let him forget it. Joe Pepitone, talented in so many areas, developed a perfect imitation of the walk.

The next time Bobby comes out to the mound to remove a pitcher, see if you can still see why the organist chose that song.

There was one player who didn't surprise anybody when he became a manager. The only question was whether or not Felipe Alou would get a chance. When we traded for him shortly after the start of the 1971 season, he was already 36 years old, on the downside of a good career that began in 1958, the first year the Giants moved west. During that time, of course, he played in an all-Alou outfield with his brothers Matty and Jesus. For part of 1973, he was reunited on the Yankees with Matty.

In one game with us, he hit a chopper down the line that eluded the third baseman. He went full-tilt right out of the box and slid into second with a double on a ball that most guys would have been satisfied with a single. Ralph Houk said, "Hey, guys, that's a ballplayer!" I was impressed. Many, many players get a hit and lope down to first. He was full-speed from the first step. That's why you can't judge a player just on his stats. They will never tell you which players are awake and hungry and which ones are just accepting what they are given.

Alou was a big, strong guy, but he wasn't a smooth, natural baseball player like Bobby Bonds, for instance. He had all these sort of clipped, almost awkward motions, like he had to think about everything before he did it. His batting stroke was like that: short and choppy. Rusty Torres called him "Mechanical Man." Often the players for whom the game doesn't come naturally are the ones who hustle themselves into superior careers.

I soon discovered that Felipe wasn't just a ballplayer. He was a great, warm guy, a real gentleman. I was invited to his apartment for dinner a few times. Felipe was an inspiring guy in a lot of ways, and I know the fellows who played *for* him must have thought as highly of him as those who played *with* him. Felipe had *manager* written all over him. I'm just glad baseball finally got the message in time for him to have a chance.

A Fool and His Slider Are Soon Parted

In spring training of 1968, Dooley Womack was the returning Yankees bullpen ace. The future looked bright, until Dooley himself darkened it. "It was my own damned fault. I kept begging Ralph Houk: 'Let me hit. Let me hit.' He let me hit, all right," Dooley recalls. "I hit lefty, and he let me hit against Al Jackson, a little lefty with the Mets who had about the biggest breaking curveball in baseball."

Now, in spring training you might think a fellow pitcher might ease up against another member of the hurling fraternity, throw him a little batting-practice fastball. You would be wrong.

"So here comes that curve, straight at me, but it's curving away from me, over the plate, and like a fool, I swing," Dooley says. He missed it by a considerable margin. "So, like an even bigger fool, I think I have to extend my arms to make contact." He didn't, and sat down after three pitches.

"I pitched another inning. I felt okay because I was warm. That night, I couldn't sleep because of the pain. It turns out I tore my rotator cuff *at bat!*" Womack says. "I threw 10,000 sliders as hard as I could and never had a sore arm. I swung at three curves from Al Jackson, and that was my career.

"I was in 45 games in 1968 but could hardly break a windowpane. My numbers were much worse than the year before but not as bad as they should have been, because I was fooling them," Dooley admits. "They came up looking for that hard slider or a pretty good fastball, and it took them a while to adjust to my new lack of speed. But they did. Oh, yeah.

"I rubbed this stuff on my arm every day. It was so hot it burned the skin off," Dooley remembers. "What it did was, it got me to focus on the burning on the skin, rather than the pain in my shoulder. That's the only way I could pitch through it."

Manager Ralph Houk came up to Womack in private and asked, "What's the matter?"

"Nothing," Dooley said.

"Yes, there is," the old catcher insisted. "Your fastball's a few inches short." A few feet was more like it.

"You didn't tell anybody about injuries in those days," Dooley says. "There were no guaranteed contracts. I took some cortisone shots. They helped with the pain but not the velocity. I needed everything I had behind every pitch, and I couldn't do it anymore."

At the end of the season, the Yankees traded him to the Astros. It was there he came to appreciate Houk even more.

"Houk was a player's manager. He worked with you. He was a good all-around guy," Womack remembers fondly. "He was like Joe Torre, in that he would take the press heat for the players. When I got to the Astros, Harry Walker was just the opposite. He would come up to one of his players in the on-deck circle and put his arm around him like he was teaching him or consoling him. The players hated that." It tells the whole crowd that something is wrong and implies that the manager has the answer, if only the dumb player would get the message.

In August Dooley became part of baseball literary history when he was traded to the one-year Seattle Pilots for Jim Bouton, who wrote all about it and everything else in his famous book, *Ball Four*. He lasted one more year, in Oakland, before he concluded that, even though his stat line never looked that bad, he just wasn't going to be able to do it anymore. His arm wasn't going to come back.

"I came home and had my arm sewn up," Dooley says. "They took eight stitches, but I never tried to rehab. I knew I was done. Years later, a doctor looked at my arm and said, 'You don't even *have* a rotator cuff!' No kidding. They wanted me to have another surgery, but I told them I didn't need to throw sliders any more at my age. As long as I can shake hands and lift a fork, I'll be fine."

In 1968 one game proved clearly that Womack's stuff might not have been as good as the previous year, yet it also proved how curious baseball outcomes can be.

He was pitching in the eighth inning of a 4–3 game against the Twins, started by Jim Bouton. Womack relieved John Wyatt, who stopped with the Yankees for only seven games on his way from Boston to Detroit. Wyatt walked Killebrew and Oliva to start the inning. Houk waved for Dooley.

Bobby Cox, now known as the Braves' manager for the last century or so, was the Yankees' third baseman, his only year of regular employ as a player. He hit .229 with no power, which is why it was his only year. He booted Rich Rollins' grounder. A run scored. Bob Allison walked, bringing up catcher John Roseboro.

Roseboro helped convince Womack his stuff wasn't what it used to be. "Roseboro hit a line drive back to the box so hard it *stuck to my leg!* I had time to reach down and grab it before it hit the ground!" Dooley says, still wincing in recall. "I threw to Bobby at third. He threw to Mickey at first. Triple play!" He got three outs on one of the hardest balls ever hit against him.

"The Yankee PR people always told me that when the team turned the next triple play, they would have me back as a guest, make a big deal out of it," Dooley says. "They better hurry up. It's been 40 years."

You Can Look It Up

I played 15 years and got into 1,881 games. I didn't set the record book on fire, but I brushed up against it a few times.

In 1971 I became the first Yankee to play an entire season without making an error. My streak was 204 in all, from making a throw to second on a Jim Price single versus Detroit that got by the second baseman, to an error against the White Sox 50 games into the 1972 season. About two weeks later, Al Kaline made a bad throw, ending his record-setting 242 consecutive games as an outfielder. He, Bill Freehan, and Norm Cash all made errors against the Orioles, helping them to a 15–3 win. I bet those three guys never made errors in the same game before or after.

Errors are such a subjective thing. Official scorers vary a lot from team to team and season to season. A lot of the games I see today make me wonder what you have to do to get an error! Other times it seems like no mercy is shown. I remember a game where it was sunny, but there was still a little rain off and on; very unusual. I was wearing sunglasses, and somebody hit a high fly. I flipped down the glasses, but raindrops hit the lenses, and I couldn't see for a second. The ball dropped after hitting the side of my glove. I got an error, a run scored, and I felt bad. Mel Stottlemyre had been shutting them out, and it was very close. But he didn't allow any more runs, and we held on.

Lights at night are worse than the sun in the daylight. Memorial Stadium in Baltimore was the worst, especially in left center. Paul Blair was an even better center fielder than everybody thinks, having to deal with those lights.

I hit two home runs in the same game six times. Strangely enough, five of those times I switch-hit the homers: one batting lefty, one righty. It's easier to tell you the time I *didn't* switch-hit them: June 1973, both against Gaylord Perry.

What I'm told is far rarer than switching homers is switching triples, which I did once against the Senators back in 1970. I suspect I hold the record for switch-hitting triples against pitchers with the combined most letters in their last names: Shellenback and Gogolewski.

Even though I have a reputation as a quiet player whose contributions to winning didn't always get a lot of attention, I did have one guy pretty loudly in my corner: Phil Rizzuto. He was always one of my biggest supporters in the announcing booth. Phil always said I was the best he'd seen at playing the odd angles and shadows in left field of Yankee Stadium. He always said I made the best catches out there. He was very complimentary to me.

One of Phil's best-known attributes, however, was a complete fabrication. He had a reputation, as they say, of tossing quarters around like they were manhole covers. But I remember one night at Trader Vic's Polynesian restaurant in Toronto, I was having dinner by myself. When I asked for the check, the waiter said the man over in the corner had just picked it up. There was Phil, sitting there completely unnoticed. And this wasn't picking up the check for a rookie. This was well into the 1970s, when I was established. It also wasn't the only time it happened. That was the kind of guy he was. He was genuine. I never saw him angry or even in a bad mood. I loved the guy. To me, he was a great person.

Even Phil might not have known, but I do hold one American League record, the most sacrifice flies in one year: 17 in 1971. Bobby Bonilla tied me in 1996 with the Orioles. They didn't have sacrifice flies before 1954, when somebody decided that scoring a run by hitting a fly ball was both worthy and intentional. I'd have to agree. It is important to get that run, and a hitter will succeed more often if he just tries to get the ball into the outfield somehow, than if he tries to get a hit.

Gil Hodges hit 19 the first year they kept track, and that is still the major-league record. Before I hit 17, the previous American league record was 12. So I didn't just break the record, I murdered it. Move over, Barry.

The previous record was held by Jimmy Piersall, Jackie Jensen, Minnie Minoso, Vic Power, and Jorge's uncle, Leo Posada. The only reason I know all this is because of my friend and former Yankees public-relations director, Marty Appel.

"I love baseball history, certainly more than the players do, so I always tried to force-feed it to them," Marty tells. "One year I gave all the postgame interview guests a copy of *Total Baseball.*" Marty was a baseball geek before they called them that. For instance, Marty was a technical advisor to Billy Crystal's HBO movie, *61**, about Mantle and Maris as they pursued Ruth's home-run record in 1961. Tom Candiotti, a knuckleball pitcher for several teams in the 1980s and 1990s, was cast in the role of knuckleball pitcher Hoyt Wilhelm. When Candiotti takes the mound as Wilhelm, he tilts his head to one side, just as Wilhelm did. That tilt of the head is courtesy of Marty Appel's attention to detail.

"Early in my Yankee days, I thought that the players would like a trophy or a plaque for a milestone or a record," Marty says. "After all, you get nothing for leading the league in any department, other than a line in the record book. So I had my friend Jack Danzis, who had a trophy business in Lyndhurst, New Jersey, make plaques that had photos and captions celebrating various events. I remember we honored Felipe Alou's 2,000th hit. Then, in 1971, I stumbled on Roy's having a chance to set the league sacrifice-fly record. I made a sketch of what Roy's commemorative plaque should look like and say and gave it to Jack.

"I started priming the team for the record-breaking fly, by making a fuss, as he neared the record, that he would never break it because no pitcher would throw him a strike in that situation and risk being known forever as the man who gave up the record-setting sacrifice fly," Marty says, laughing.

Of course, I finally got it in the first inning against the White Sox and Tommy John, late in July. "Yes, it finally happened," Marty says. "An announcement on the scoreboard was all we did on that day. When the plaque was finished, I gave it to him, and I think he liked it a lot. It might have been the first award he'd gotten, though, of course, he eventually got those two World Series rings."

Yes, I did like it. Marty was, and is, a very thoughtful person who appreciates the big and the little things a player does to win. Funny, after a while I became well known for not being well known. From the glamorous players still with the Yankees when I arrived to the down years that followed to the volatile 1970s, I was the guy who showed up every day and did his job. Bill James, the Babe Ruth of baseball geeks, once wrote an article comparing my career favorably to Jim Rice's. It was controversial, and I would be the last person to compare one player's career to another that way. But it was good to know that he appreciated and saw the value in a player who helped win games with speed, defense, a good eye, and enough power to drive the ball and keep the defense honest.

It means something to me to have been the only player to bridge the gap between the last years of Mickey and Whitey and the winning teams of the 1970s. For a few years, I wondered if we would ever turn the corner. When we did, it was a great thrill and honor to be there, but it was always great to be in the Yankees dugout, from Mantle all the way to Rivers.

It Gets Late Early

"It gets late early" is one of Yogi Berra's most famous "Yogisms," and, like many of them, it says a lot with a little. I ought to know, because it refers to what was my office for 15 years: left field in Yankee Stadium. Yogi admits, "I really didn't say everything I said," but this one is real and critical at World Series time.

Yogi Berra's unique sayings, or "Yogisms," have become famous over the years. One of them, "It gets late early," couldn't be more apt.

I bet Yogi first made this astute observation in the fall, because that is about the time it gets late early in Yankee Stadium. Left field in Yankee Stadium is a horrible sun field even today. It was a lot worse before the renovations in 1976, when they moved home plate back 30 feet and changed the angle slightly. We used to be thankful for the air pollution in the Bronx because it cut down the glare. Too bad I didn't play in an earlier generation, when a few thousand fans smoking cigarettes might have added to the helpful haze.

By the seventh or eighth inning of any day game, the sun would start to come down exactly in my line of vision. It would disappear for a time behind the upper deck, but then, like the monster in the horror movie that always appears one more time after you think he's dead, it would appear suddenly once again. There it was, between the decks of the stadium, when you least expected it.

As the season wore on, it got worse. By August, it would be in your eyes for maybe half the game. By October, it was just about the entire game. That bright, crisp October sky is beautiful to everybody but the left fielder. The haze, pollution, and smoke burn away, leaving him unprotected and often nearly blind. Back when the World Series was played during the day, the left fielder was in trouble from the playing of the national anthem.

What Yogi was describing so succinctly was that, during the regular season, the sun gets in the left fielder's eyes late in the game, but, as the season wears on, it is a problem for a longer duration. It gets late early.

Gene Woodling, one of the few players to be part of the five consecutive World Series winners from 1949 to1953, believed that the sun in left field was a Yankees advantage. He learned to play it, as I did, because he was there day after day. National League left fielders were often, well, blindsided.

In 1971 I played 145 games in left field and didn't make an error. But that didn't mean I didn't have some harrowing experiences and narrow escapes. At least I didn't suffer the fate of Norm Siebern.

Siebern was a Minor League Player of the Year in 1957 and hit .300 as a Yankees rookie the next year. He even won a Golden Glove for his play in left field in the second year the award was given. The other American League outfield winners were Jimmy Piersall and Al Kaline, both among the best outfielders of all time. The defensive statistics now in use were then unknown. They show Siebern was barely more than average defensively, but because Golden Gloves voting is notoriously fickle, he probably got it as much for being a rookie who had a decent year at bat as for his glove.

It got late early for Norm in the sixth and eighth innings of Game 4 of the 1958 World Series, when, though he was not charged with errors, he looked uncertain on two fly balls that fell for base hits. A run scored each inning and the Yanks lost 3–0. Siebern took the fall for the loss, though one might consider that Warren Spahn's pitching a two-hit shutout might have had something to do with it, too.

As a teenager in California, I watched Siebern's struggles on television, not dreaming that I would be fighting that same sun for a living in a few short years. In the next game, Elston Howard replaced Siebern and made a diving catch on a Red Schoendienst liner and then doubled up the runner. His great play, coming so soon after Siebern's poor ones, only emphasized the difference in their defensive abilities. Norm was seen no more in that World Series.

He wasn't seen very much longer in a Yankees uniform, either. He fell to .271 in 1959, a year the Yankees finished third and many players had off years. A bit more than a year after his World Series failure, he was bundled with a few others and traded to Kansas City. He had some very good years there, but the trade is known mostly for the outfielder the Yankees got in return: Roger Maris.

From 1968 through 1972, my prime years before my hamstrings started barking, I made only eight errors, fewer than two a year, playing full-time left field and half those games in the sun field of New York. For my entire career I fielded .988. For comparison, Barry Bonds' fielding average, at least as I write this, is .984. If I could reach it, I caught it.

Of course, as Yogi might say, not all my errors were mistakes. At least not in my mind. When the designated hitter debuted in 1973, I was sorry for one reason: it kept Tommy Davis in the league. His legs were gone, but he was designated hitting for Baltimore and remained a guy who made his living hitting vicious line drives to left field. One day, he hit one right at me, at least at first. Then it disappeared into the lights. When that happens, you just try to get to the right spot, because you will usually pick it up again in a split second, with time to recover. Not this time. I never saw it again until it hit me on the shoulder and caromed away from me. Davis stopped at third with a triple.

At least I thought it was a triple. Then the *E* flashed on the scoreboard. How can you make an error on a ball you can't see? I'm sure Davis agreed with me, as his triple became just another time at bat. I can't complain too much. I was lucky it didn't hit me in the head.

I was luckier than Davis a few years earlier in the second game of a doubleheader against the White Sox at the stadium. The sun was low, and I hit one into the left center-field gap. Ken Berry, who at the time was about as fast and sure-handed as anyone playing center, ranged after it. I thought it was in his pocket. It hit him in the shoulder. I could tell from the way he moved that he never saw it. It got late early for him. I guess the scorer figured if Ken Berry couldn't catch it, it must be a hit, and I got a double or triple to show for it. The sun giveth, and the sun taketh away.

I thought I might cost Ron Guidry a game a few years later when Al Oliver sliced one down the left-field line. If you have seen the film of that famous World Series catch that Sandy Amoros made off Yogi in 1955, then you will have seen something similar to what Al hit to me, except Oliver's was more of a line drive. Running to my right, I was looking straight into the sun, flying blind. I ran to where I thought it would be and guessed slightly wrong. It hit me in the shoulder, and a run came in. I was very glad when we rallied to win the game.

Sometimes you're fighting more than just the sun out there. I remember a game around 1974, also against the White Sox, with Bill Melton hitting. He led the league in homers one year and hit high, high fly balls. It was the first inning of a twilight double-header, when it wasn't quite dark, the lights weren't on, and what sun was left was surprisingly bright if you looked at it wrong.

Melton hit one of his mortar shots to left center. It was so high I had plenty of time to camp under it. So did Bobby Murcer in center. We looked away from the sun, but in the gray of twilight, the ball looked like the same color as the sky, like it did when you looked up at that roof in the Metrodome in Minneapolis. I looked up and saw nothing but sky. Bobby didn't see it, either. It fell about 30 feet behind us, and Melton was standing on third. I got the error!

Maury Allen was the scorer, and later I asked him, "How is that an error?"

He said, "It was a catchable ball."

Right. If you see it.

chapter 8
In the Big Inning

*Roy White, pictured here
early in his Yankees career,
grew up playing sock ball
in Compton, California.*
Photo courtesy of Roy White.

Straight Outta Compton

I lived on 131ˢᵗ street in Compton, California. The three Neal brothers lived the next street over. There were always enough guys around to have some sort of game. One day we'd play at our house and the next day at somebody else's, with different ground rules. We played doubleheaders every day. Sometimes tripleheaders! We all switch-hit, imitating our favorite players. We used a tightly rolled-up sock, with which we could throw some nasty curves.

When the other kids weren't around, I hit rocks with a stick. I'd imagine two teams, go down the lineups, and play complete games in my head, all with just a stick and a rock. Sometimes in the ninth inning, I would pinch-hit for Ed Lopat or Clem Labine. I usually hit a home run.

But sock ball didn't get me to the majors. Or Reggie Smith, or Don Wilson, or Lenny Randle, Ron Woods, Dave Nelson, Al Cowens, Wayne Simpson, or Lonnie Smith, all of whom, in addition to me, made the majors by way of Compton. We all made it by virtue of our talent and commitment. I attended Centennial High School. About 10 years after I came along, across town, Compton High School had *four* players who made the majors on the same team: Dick Davis, Gary Ward, Odell Jones, and Reggie Walton. Maybe none would have made it without Charles Siler.

Mr. Siler had played in the Negro Leagues as a young man, one of many for whom making the major leagues was only a dream in those pre–Jackie Robinson years. After his career was over, he moved west to Compton and opened a dry-cleaning business across the street from the park. He noticed that there were a lot of kids like me who played baseball, or something like baseball, every waking moment but who had no real fields to play on and not much in the way of organized leagues.

Charles Siler changed all that. His son Michael remembers, "Dad didn't have any help at first, but eventually he organized leagues for players at every age group."

There was a Willy Mays League for the youngest kids, ages eight to 10. Then there was a Koufax, a Mantle, and a Connie Mack League, for kids up to 18 years old. I started playing in Mr. Siler's Mickey Mantle League. Little did I know that a few years later I'd be playing the outfield next to Mickey!

In the 1970s and early 1980s, when several of my local buddies and I were big leaguers or had been recently, Compton boasted that it produced the most major-league players of any city in the world. But there haven't been any big leaguers from Compton High or Centennial High in some years. There may be some complicated sociological reasons, but for Michael Siler, the reason is simple.

"Dad got sick," he says. "There was nobody to take his place. I'm not saying he was a one-man operation, but he did a lot and was the driving force. There were always obstacles, even when his leagues were going well. It was hard to raise money, though several local businesses eventually helped. There was endless fund-raising for keeping the fields in good shape, for travel and uniforms. Then, after it was successful, everybody wanted a piece of it."

There is new hope for whatever sock-ball players there might be in Compton now. Major League Baseball has put a project there to help develop young players. Darrell Miller, who used to play for the Angels, heads it up. Darrell is the baseball brother of the basketball Millers, Cheryl and Reggie.

After I was finished with Mr. Siler's leagues, I went on to play American Legion ball and high school ball. I played basketball and football, too. Baseball began right after basketball ended. The coach called me right out of class for a game. I played varsity in 10th grade, which was pretty rare. Our shortstop was Dave Kelly. He was All-League, a little older, and our inspiration. He signed with the Tigers for $50,000. I played against him in the Southern League a few years later. He was with Montgomery when I was with Columbus. I thought he couldn't miss, but it's more difficult than you think when you're a kid.

Because of Kelly, scouts came to our games, and eventually they started coming up to me. They were bird dogs, not scouts, local guys who were connected to scouts. If a scout signed a player a bird dog suggested, the dog might get a small fee, but usually they just dogged for the love of the game and to show that they could recognize talent. I was playing four games a week by my senior year. I knew three or four teams were interested. I saw guys from the Reds, Dodgers, and Houston Colt .45s [now Astros]. I had no idea the Yankees were interested. I never saw a Yankees scout.

So it was a shock when I was playing in a summer league after I had graduated and a Yankees scout knocked on our door. His name was Tuffie Hashem. You don't forget a name like that. He had a contract and was ready to sign me. He was the first one who delivered a real offer.

I was a pretty good student and had a baseball scholarship to UCLA lined up. Long Beach State wanted me for football, but that was out of the question. At maybe 170 pounds, I'd get killed. But I figured if nobody came around, I'd take the baseball scholarship. Who knows, I might have played with Chris Chambliss, who went from junior-college running back to UCLA first baseman just a few years after I might have been there.

But Tuffie made a good case for me turning pro right then, not the least successful argument being that I'd make some money, which came in more than handy for my mom and my siblings. There were no short-season rookie leagues back then, so I didn't get started until the next year.

No player makes the big leagues on his own. Every one of us has family, friends, coaches, and others helping us and rooting for us. I think maybe the Compton kids, since Mr. Siler let go of his leagues, haven't had enough support. Maybe with Major League Baseball taking an interest, more support is on the way. Maybe Centennial High will add to its list of big-league players once again.

A First Baseman by Any Other Name

I was pretty excited when the Dodgers moved near my Compton, California, home in 1958. I was a teenage baseball fanatic. I remember watching Wally Moon hit his "Moon Shots" over that strange left-field screen at the Los Angeles Coliseum, where it was only 250 feet. What I didn't appreciate was how frustrated Duke Snider was, trying to hit homers to right, where it was 440! That's what happens when you try to play baseball on a football field. If I had played there, I think I might have hit only righty.

I was a fan of local teams well before the Dodgers. The Los Angeles Angels and Hollywood Stars of the Pacific Coast League were only a small step below the majors. A lot of players in the PCL then would be regulars in the majors if they played now, after expansion. I remember a lot of guys who later played for the Pirates, Cubs, and Cardinals, from Dick Stuart to Bobby Del Greco. I remember two in particular.

Carlos Bernier was a very fast center fielder for the Hollywood Stars and made it to the Pirates for one year. In fact, he was the first black player on the Pirates, in 1953. He hit only .213 and was back in the coast league the next year. He led that league in stolen bases three times and in 2004 was elected to the Pacific Coast League Hall of Fame. When I was a kid, I wondered why he didn't play in the majors.

Later I realized that, though Jackie Robinson broke the color line in the majors in 1947, he didn't blow it wide open. There was still plenty of room to discriminate. The Pirates in 1953 were lousy. Plenty of young players in addition to Bernier had bad years but were given other chances. But Carlos had more than a low batting average working against him. He was black, he was Puerto Rican, and he was aggressive.

Vic Power, Roberto Clemente, Orlando Cepeda, and others can tell you being a Latin ballplayer in the 1950s, and even later, was tough. The language barrier and cultural differences could be harder to solve than Warren Spahn's curve. Bernier didn't make it any easier by not only running the bases aggressively, but occasionally confronting other players and umpires. He had a running feud with Angels infielder Gene Mauch. Known as a mild-mannered major-league manager, he was pretty fiery as a player and was not above throwing dirt in the sliding Bernier's face as Carlos stole second base.

I enjoyed watching Bernier and was glad he played for my local team. Now I realize he almost certainly had the ability to play in the major leagues had the way not been quite so uphill for him.

The other guy I rooted for was a big, slow, right-handed slugger named Steve Bilko. He led the PCL in homers three years in a row in the mid-1950s and probably made more money than if he had been riding the bench in the majors. He was usually listed at 6'1", 240 pounds, but that might have been a little tall and a little thin, from what I remember. This was a big guy for any era, but he was extraordinarily large for his time. He had a huge hitch in his swing, which might have been why he thrived in the minors but couldn't stick in the big leagues. He didn't have time to hitch against the really good pitchers.

He was the regular Cardinals first baseman in 1953 and hit 21 homers. He also led the league with 125 strikeouts, back when strikeouts were considered shameful and more than 60 or so were nearly intolerable. Mickey Mantle took terrible abuse from New York writers for his high strikeout totals in the 1950s, and he struck out more than 125 in only one season. Of course, Steve Bilko was no Mickey Mantle. Still, he was our own local slugger and very popular around town. He even had a brief, though typically unsuccessful, shot with the new Los Angeles Dodgers in 1958.

Incidentally, that 1957 Angels team had a lot of baseball smarts. In addition to Mauch, it featured a good-fielding, no-hit second baseman named George "Sparky" Anderson, and a left-handed curveball pitcher named Tommy Lasorda.

One of my favorite television shows when I was a kid, and one of the most popular ones on the air, was *The Phil Silvers*

Show, better known as *Sergeant Bilko*. Broadway comedian Phil Silvers played Sgt. Bilko, an army lifer who was forever running scams on his fellow soldiers. Baseball stars such as Yogi Berra sometimes were guests on the show, which made it even more fun for me to watch.

In 1960 Steve Bilko got one last chance to play in the majors, after I thought his fate as a minor-league slugger was sealed. The Detroit Tigers drafted him and platooned him at first with their young lefty, Norm Cash. Steve hit all of .207, but his enthusiasm made him a fan favorite. Tigers announcer Ernie Harwell quickly started calling him "Big Sarge" after the television Bilko.

Only much later did I learn that the writer of the Bilko show lived in L.A. and was, like me, a big Hollywood Stars and Los Angeles Angels fan. Nat Hiken's favorite player was the big first baseman, and that is why he named his wheeler-dealer sergeant after Steve.

So Steve Bilko's nickname was inspired by a TV character inspired by Steve Bilko! This has to be the only case in baseball history where a player was nicknamed after himself.

Campy's Little Curves

When people ask me when I became a switch-hitter, I don't know what to tell them. I don't remember ever being anything else. Back in my neighborhood when I was a kid, we had a field all marked out. Over the chicken coop was a homer. We met every Saturday and played the Game of the Week. If the game was Yankees versus Indians, we'd go through the lineup, imitating each batter's stance: McDougald, Collins, Bauer, Berra, then Avila, Mitchell, Doby, and Rosen.

If the hitter was lefty, you hit lefty. If righty, you hit righty. Switch-hitting seemed natural to me. We all did it. Reggie Smith was the Little League home-run champ of the Compton, California, Boys League two years after I played in it, and I suspect he learned to switch-hit the same way I did.

Bert Campaneris was a professional switch-hitter for over 20 years and a switch-pitcher for two innings. Photo courtesy of Getty Images.

When I started playing on the school team, though, I just hit righty, my natural side. I was hitting only about .250 and was getting frustrated. I asked the coach if I could hit lefty in practice and started hitting line drives. That was it. I was a switcher from that day on. All my coaches encouraged it. It also put me a little closer to first base, where my speed helped beat out grounders. That extra step is probably why I hit nine points better for my career from the left side, though my slugging average and on-base percentage is a little better lefty, too. I think this is simply because a switch-hitter naturally hits more often from the left side.

There was one day, early in my career, that being a switch-hitter was a little more complicated than all the other days. That is, what happens when a switch-hitter meets a switch-pitcher?

Bert "Campy" Campaneris was the star shortstop of the Oakland A's in the early 1970s and a great all-around athlete. He is one of the very few players to hit two homers in his first major-league game. Late in 1965, his second year in the majors, he played a different position every inning against the Angels. He even pitched the eighth inning, giving up a run on two walks and a single by Joe Adcock.

The A's had the cellar all to themselves that year and were drawing crowds that were often no more than two or three thousand. Announcing Campy's stunt attracted a crowd of more than 20,000, so from that aspect it was a success. The A's won the publicity game that day but lost the baseball game 5–3 in 13 innings. Campy's run contributed to the loss, but when a team loses 103 games and finishes 43 games out of first, that one run he gave up didn't make much difference. Most of the players who became the excellent Swinging A's were still several years from the majors.

When I heard of Campy's stunt, I was not surprised. He had done the same thing three years earlier against my team, the Fort Lauderdale Yankees of the Florida State League. Against us, he didn't just play a different position every inning, pitching one; he pitched two innings and faced right-handed batters pitching with his right hand and left-handed batters using his left! He didn't try that on the big-league mound.

You have a better chance of seeing a perfect game or an unassisted triple play than seeing a pitcher use both hands. It has been done only once in the majors since 1893, when Greg Harris pitched an ambidextrous inning for the Expos late in 1995. Like the A's, the Expos were in last place, and manager Felipe Alou thought it might liven things up a bit. Harris had been begging for the chance for years. He even had a special glove made.

Harris pitched the ninth inning of a 9–7 loss to the Reds. A career right-hander, he pitched lefty to catcher Ed Taubensee, who obligingly tapped a little grounder that the catcher fielded and threw to first to complete this history-making play.

In 2007 the Yankees used their 45th draft choice to pick a hurler from Creighton University who is an ambidextrous pitcher for real, not just for publicity. Pat Venditte has been a successful college pitcher, mostly in relief, and throws with equal effectiveness with either hand. However, his level of effectiveness is unlikely to find its way to the majors, as players drafted 45th rarely make it to the bigs. Another ambidextrous pitcher, Matt Brunnig of Harvard University, has also been scouted. It has also been said that President Truman switched hands from year to year in throwing out the ceremonial first pitch.

So although Campy's switch-pitching is rare, a switch-pitcher facing a switch-hitter is even rarer. As far as I know, I'm the only hitter in professional baseball to have done it, though perhaps somebody back in 1893 beat me to it by a century or so.

It was August 13, 1962. Campy started the fourth inning on the mound. Fort Lauderdale was ahead 8–4, thanks to an RBI single by Ian Dixon, followed by a three-run homer by Dave Turnbull. Campy walked two but also struck out two, including Dixon.

Campaneris was known during his big-league career as having a strong arm at shortstop, so he threw plenty hard for the Florida State League. "While I was on deck, I remember thinking,

'Boy, he throws hard,'" Dixon remembers. "I didn't want to strike out, but he got me."

The next inning, Campy returned to the mound. The first hitter was our pitcher, Gary Lewis, who was left-handed all the way. To everyone's surprise, Campy put his glove on his right hand and pitched lefty! Lewis wasn't much of a hitter, even for a pitcher. He hit all of .116 that year. But he did have a bit of an eye and would take a walk if the pitcher were so generous as to offer one. Lewis walked. I was hitting leadoff and was on deck.

There was talk on the bench from the time Campaneris entered the game that I might get a lick at him. What would I do? What would he do? I noticed that while he threw hard right-handed, he didn't have much else. From the left side, he threw much more slowly and even had a little slow curve. I didn't think too much about it. When I got to the plate, he had the ball in his right hand, so I just got in right-handed. He threw hard, and I hit it hard. A double, the only hit he gave up.

Now, if you talk to Dixon and my teammates, they will tell you a story that has grown around this at-bat. They remember that I stood in righty, then changed to lefty, so Campy changed hands, and that this went on, back and forth, for some time, driving the umpire nuts, until he made me choose one of the batter's boxes and stay there. Never happened. I think they are just remembering the conversation on the bench, when they speculated what *might* happen. I stood in. He pitched. I doubled.

The next two hitters, Bill Burke and Mike Hegan, were both lefties, and he struck out both of them! Using that little dinky curve that, as Dizzy Dean used to say, "dropped from the want of speed."

"I was surprised that lefties struck out against Campaneris," remembered Dixon in an article by Len Corben in the *North Shore* (Vancouver) *Outlook* a few years ago. "Because he just couldn't throw hard enough that way. All he had was this little gravity curveball."

Hegan was particularly annoyed at striking out. Guess what star shortstop, with whom Hegan played for two years in Oakland, never let him forget?

In 2004 Turnbull and Dixon organized a reunion of the 1962 Fort Lauderdale team. Everybody was telling lies and having a great time. Then Dixon told a lie that I didn't think was funny. He was telling everybody I struck out against Campaneris! I'm a mild-mannered guy, but get the record straight. I told him about the hit, emphatically. Then he started laughing, knowing he got my goat. Now every time I see those broken-down old scrubeenies, they tell me I struck out, and I got to tell everybody the truth *and* do it calmly and coolly, or else they just laugh all the harder.

I Was a Baseball Zombie

I wasn't really a baseball zombie. Art Lopez was a baseball zombie. Sort of.

The first few years I went to spring training in Tampa I was just a kid, a couple of years out of high school. Tampa in the early 1960s was definitely what you would call pre–Civil Rights. All the black players (not that there were many) stayed in the black section of town. As a Californian, I didn't know what to expect down South, but a lot of it wasn't good. Perhaps the expectations that there was something for me to fear around the next corner made this zombie business possible in the first place.

There wasn't a whole lot to do in Tampa in those days in *any* section of town. What were a bunch of young guys to do, other than annoy each other with the silliest practical jokes and jibes imaginable? Although everything was new to me, some of the other guys seemed like wise veterans, though in reality they were only a few years older.

Art Lopez was my Tampa roommate. He was about seven years older and was born in Puerto Rico, but he went to college in New Jersey; so, compared to me, he had been around.

"Roy was a serious-minded guy back then, just like he is now," says Art. "But it was pretty unusual to be that serious among the young guys trying to make a big-league baseball team. Roy would go back to the room really early, get into bed, and read one of those magazines full of baseball statistics until he fell asleep. Some of us decided Roy needed to loosen up a little."

At one time, Artie was being groomed for the Yankees outfield, but those few years he had on me worked against him. When he was my age, Mickey Mantle, Roger Maris, and Tom Tresh seemed as if they would be the Yankees outfield forever. They weren't, but it must have seemed like forever to Art.

He competed for an outfield spot against guys with big swings and big hopes from the front office, such as Don Lock and Roger Repoz. Not exactly household names today, but in Art's day they got more attention than his speed and place-hitting did. He didn't fit the Yankees power image. Every year he'd go to spring training, almost make the team, get sent to the minors, and have a great year, only to see it repeated again and again.

He also missed out on the expansion of 1969, which gave chances to a lot of players who had been overlooked. Lou Piniella, for instance, always called himself an expansion player. He failed to impress Baltimore and Cleveland as a very young player, but he established himself as a hard-hitting regular thanks to the new Kansas City Royals. But by then, Art was well over the baseball hill.

We both got a taste of big-league coffee in 1965. While I was barely old enough to vote, Art was 28. That's ancient for a big-league rookie. It was to be his only taste of the majors, though he played for several more years in the minors, during which, among other things, he played for the world-famous Toledo Mud Hens, the Yankees' Triple A farm club at the time. The Hens then played at a refurbished county-fair racetrack. Rumor had it that the refurbishing was somewhat incomplete, as the olfactory memory of decades of horses remained in the clubhouses. "The outfield was full of pebbles," Art remembers. Little wonder, since it had been a racetrack only a few months before Lopez arrived.

He also played several years in Japan, one of the first real American success stories there.

But in Tampa, Art was the wise veteran, and I was the kid. I was also the fall guy. One night he and Dave Turnbull—a big, strong guy whose home-run swing was never seen in big-league ballparks—snuck into my room before I arrived.

"We were on the road. It was hot in Daytona Beach, even during spring training, and those hotels were old even then," says Lopez. "We got two whole dollars a day for meal money. So most afternoons everybody just went out for a hamburger, then we all went our separate ways for the evening. We knew that Roy would go straight back to his room and his baseball magazines.

"There was no air conditioning, just those big, lazy ceiling fans. So everybody kept their windows open. I stole some ketchup from a cafeteria. Dave and I climbed in through Roy's open window. Dave went into the bathroom with a bucket of water and closed the door. There was a big brass bed, and right next to the bed was a closet. I hid in the closet and poured ketchup on my arm and waited. It wasn't too long before Roy came in and settled into bed with his magazine. Then he turned off the lights to sleep. That was our cue. I stuck my 'bloody' arm out of the closet and reached toward Roy's head and made some deep, what I hoped to be scary, moans."

I heard some crazy sound, turned on the light, and saw this bloody arm above my head. I jumped out of bed and ran toward the bathroom.

It is said that I screamed.

I opened the bathroom door. There was Turnbull with his bucket.

Perhaps I screamed again. Then my eyes focused, and I saw who it was. They had a most jolly time. I was just relieved that it was these morons and not some, well, whatever it might have been. Their idiot prank was soon the talk of spring training, at least among the rookies.

Did it loosen me up? Who knows? I still turned in early and studied baseball magazines every night, but I was happy to know my teammates thought enough about me that they felt the need to save me from the possibly detrimental results of excessive seriousness.

Forever after, this has come to be known as "the Zombie Story," and I am still reminded of it by Art and the others at every possible opportunity. But we are all much older now and not as easily scared. Not by zombies, not by the New York Yankees spring-training camp, and not by whatever else might have challenged a young black man in Florida more than 40 years ago.

chapter 9

From DH to DL

Ron Blomberg, seen here smacking the ball in a June 1, 1973, game, was the first designated hitter in baseball history.

More than a Fastball

"Sudden" Sam McDowell is just a year older than I am, but he reached the majors four years sooner by virtue of being able to throw the ball through a brick wall, providing the wall was big enough for him to hit. He was capable of striking out more than 300 batters in a season, which he did twice, and of walking more than 130, which he did three times. Like most guys from our generation, the Yankees were special to him, even if he didn't play for them.

"I was from Pittsburgh, but I had never been to Yankee Stadium until I came to the majors," Sam remembers. He started one game at the end of the 1961 season at age 18, but didn't visit New York until the beginning of the following year. "It was a night game, but I was so excited about playing there for the first time, I arrived at 9:30 in the morning." Of course, nobody was there except security guards. "Nobody recognized me. I couldn't get in. I had to go back to the hotel and wait for the game. When I finally got to play with the Yankees, years later, my arm was hanging by a thread. I was finished, but it was still a thrill to put on the uniform."

McDowell's special ability brought him to the majors at a young age, though he had trouble sticking. In both 1962 and 1963, Sam made the big club out of spring training, only to be sent back to the minors. He believes, however, that his amazing fastball also kept him from developing as a real pitcher. "Birdie Tebbetts called all the pitches from the dugout, and he never called for anything but fastballs. Nobody tried to teach me the science of pitching, changing speeds, throwing in and out, and so on. They'd see my heat, and that's all they wanted to know about me. I was more than a fastball."

Finally, Sam was fed up. "I was out of options in 1964, and I was 7–0, starting the year in Triple A in the Pacific Coast League with Portland. I told them not to bring me up, let me stay in the minors all year. Then I'd be a free agent, and I'd sign with another team, if all they were going to do with me was have Tebbetts call fastballs."

Indians General Manager Gabe Paul told him, "You can't demand that. I'll bury you so deep in the minors you'll never find your way back."

"I don't care," Sam said. He continues, "That evening I pitched for Portland, threw a one-hitter with 16 strikeouts, and Paul called me back and said he was bringing me to Cleveland, and he would personally tell Birdie to mix 'em up." Sam had 102 strikeouts in eight games and a 1.18 earned-run average. Gabe Paul wasn't going to let him go even if Sam wanted to throw eggs at the plate. He told Tebbetts to back off. He did, and Sam pitched better. For a while.

"One day I see our catcher, Jose Azcue, looking into the dugout every pitch, and sure enough: fastball, fastball, fastball," Sam says. "I told Paul again that I wanted out." However, by this time a Sam McDowell, even one with only one pitch, was too valuable to let go. McDowell never got Birdie to help him and doesn't believe he turned into any kind of real pitcher until Alvin Dark became manager in 1968. "Al used to let me call my own pitches. His pitching coach was Jack Sanford." Jack's best year was 1962, when he went 24–7 for Dark's Giants and came within a Willie McCovey line drive to Bobby Richardson of winning Game 7 of the World Series. "Jack couldn't break a pane of glass the last several years he pitched, but he knew *how* to pitch. He helped me have my best years."

Although Sam was correct that he needed to use his other pitches to become a complete pitcher, the best he could be, most hitters like myself were happy when he threw something besides a fastball. In my first few years, when Mantle was still in the lineup, Sam would strike him out three times using nothing but his best 100-mile-per-hour fastballs. Then he'd try to trick the rest of us with curves, like we weren't challenging enough. We always said if Sam pitched to the rest of us the way he pitched against Mantle, we wouldn't have a chance. Mantle hit .192 for his career against McDowell, striking out about 40 percent of the time and posting a slugging average not quite as high as Bobby Richardson's career mark.

Bert Blyleven was the same way, except his great pitch was the best curve I ever saw. Every time we saw him, we thought he was going to pitch a no-hitter because of that hellacious curve, and he could throw hard, too. We also thought he'd throw his arm out because of that big curve, but he never did. But somehow he'd walk a guy late in the game, then he'd try to sneak a change-up, his worst pitch, past Stick Michael or somebody, and he'd get beat. Sometimes having great physical skills can work against you or at least not be enough.

My first big-league homer was off Sam McDowell in April 1966. All of about 6,000 fans, drowning in that huge old stadium in Cleveland, saw me put one into the seats in the eighth inning. It was our only run as Sam beat us 3–1, striking out 12. I also got two singles that day, and the whole team got only seven hits.

I happened to run into a McDowell fastball, and in a strange way, it helped me. After that homer, he must have said to himself, "Okay, no more fastballs for White." He'd throw me curves and off-speed pitches, much to my relief. I'd get my hits off him. It was still no fun facing a big guy with five or six pitches, but at least I didn't have to look for that fastball.

Alvin Dark not only let Sam develop as a pitcher, but he was also known as a master strategist. One cagey move led Sam to become one of the very few left-handed second baseman in the major leagues. It came about because McDowell couldn't get Washington slugger Frank Howard out. He was the only hitter he could not throw his fastball past. "He was terrifying to watch in batting practice," Sam says. "He would walk halfway between the plate and the mound, take his stance, and have the guys throw to improve his bat speed. When he faced me, he would foul off pitches that everybody else missed. Then I'd try to get smart and fool him with a curve. I'd hang it, and he'd put it into the Virginia suburbs." So Alvin devised a cool move for the next time Howard came to bat against Sam with the game on the line.

On July 6, 1970, Sam was beating the Senators in Cleveland, 6–4, in the eighth, thanks to a Graig Nettles homer and two by Duke Sims. McDowell, as usual, hadn't gotten Howard out, yielding two singles and two walks, one intentional. Howard came up with runners on second and third and two out. Dark walked to the mound, brought in Dean Chance to pitch, pulled third baseman Nettles, moved second sacker Eddie Leon to third, and moved the lefty McDowell to second base, figuring that if Howard hit the ball, there was little chance he'd hit to Sam, because he was such a pull-hitter. Before he left the mound, Dark said to all the infielders, "Now take a look at who is playing second. If a play comes to you, *don't throw it to McDowell.*"

Sam says, "So what does Chance do? He gets behind Howard and ends up walking him intentionally. I could have done that." But then, who knows why he left Sam at second so Dean could pitch to Rick Reichardt. Maybe he felt that the righty had a better percentage against the right-handed-hitting Reichardt, who hit McDowell pretty well, too, though he was no Frank Howard.

"Of course, Reichardt hits a grounder to third, and Eddie Leon, operating on automatic pilot or something, never takes a look and throws it to second," Sam says. Howard, the 6'7", 255-pound, former Ohio State basketball center was bearing down on McDowell. "I hold it for the force. My lifetime fielding average as a second baseball is 1.000. Perfect. You can look it up." Sam returned to the mound in the ninth and struck out the side for the win.

Despite being a fine pitcher and a one-time utility infielder, McDowell was traded from the Indians one year after he won 20 games for the first time. Why? He was hurt. He went from 20 wins to 13, with every other stat also heading south. "I had a torn rotator cuff my last year in Cleveland," Sam says. "I told some writers about it. Gabe Paul called me into his office and really chewed me out. He told me, 'You don't have a sore arm! You are fine. Don't go to the papers!' He was very angry."

In the off-season, Sam discovered the reason for the anger. If the Giants had known how badly McDowell was hurt, they would never have traded Gaylord Perry for him. It looked like a trade of aces at the time, but it turned out to be more like trading a Ford 150 pickup truck for a Corvette with a burned-out engine. The fancy muscle car was dead, but the old truck just kept going.

McDowell won only 19 more games during his career. Perry won 180, including two Cy Young Awards, and pitched until he was 44. Sam was done at 32.

Sam now admits the real reason his career was shorter than most people expected, but it took him years to confront the truth. "I was an alcoholic my entire career. Yes, I knew on some level it was killing my career. Denial is so strong. When you're young, you think your talent will always be there. Sure, people tried to help me," Sam says. "When I was with the Yankees, Gabe Paul, of all people, was general manager. He secretly sent me to a psychologist. It was useless. We know now that therapy won't work if the desire to quit isn't there."

We didn't know Sam had a drinking problem when he faced us. If we did, we probably would have been even more scared to face him! It was harder for Sam to face his family. "My first wife would threaten to leave me if I didn't quit, so I'd go to AA for a month or so, get sober, and that would buy me some time. Eventually, the cycle would start again." Eventually his wife left.

Alcohol use and abuse has been part of the game probably since it began. I'd guess that the clubs that played the first games, back before the Civil War, probably had a jug of something at the end of the bench. When Jim Bouton's *Ball Four* became a bestseller in 1970, everybody thought the Yankees were a big boozing club, but McDowell disagrees, in a way. "The Yankees weren't any better or any worse than any other club. It was every club," Sam says. "'Play hard and drink hard' was the motto in every clubhouse."

By the time he hit bottom and got sober, it was too late for his baseball career but not for his life. He became, in fact, a well-regarded drug-and-alcohol counselor and helped many major-league players. He created several ongoing programs for the Texas Rangers and Toronto Blue Jays. He believes his expertise leads him to understand why steroids and other performance-enhancing drugs have become such a problem. "The owners don't understand how ballplayers think. The players think they are immortal and are so competitive they will do anything for an edge.

It is in every sport," Sam says. "The game even today doesn't have the educational programs it needs. Over 20 years ago, I brought in a doctor to talk to the Rangers. He was an M.D. and had been a champion bodybuilder. He spoke clearly about the advantages steroids give you and the health risks," Sam recalls. "It hurts everything. Every bodily function. It even affects your brain tissue. Once players really hear about how dangerous it is from another world-class athlete, they listen. But the message has to be driven home again and again."

That's how alcoholism finally began to diminish in the big leagues. Former players like Sam, Don Newcombe, and Ryne Duren went around every spring warning teams about alcohol abuse, using their own truncated careers as examples. Newcombe and Duren, despite their early successes and prodigious talents, had their last big years at age 30. The Hall of Fame that so many thought would include McDowell back in the days when he was a kid being locked out of Yankee Stadium, never called. "Players are very much better informed about nutrition and things like alcohol and amphetamines," Sam says. "Alcoholism in the big leagues is way down now. But they still don't understand how bad steroids are."

The Kibbutz Klouter

Even though his career was cut very short compared to what it might have been, I don't think anybody on the Yankees got a bigger kick out of putting on the pinstripes than Ron Blomberg. Most people today don't remember what an amazing athlete he was. Coming out of high school in Atlanta, he is still the only athlete to make the *Parade* magazine All-America teams in baseball, basketball, and football. He received well over 100 scholarship offers in both football and basketball.

"I was a 6'2" center in high school," Ron recalls. "I had a 41" vertical leap, about the same as David Thompson. I would have played forward in college. I had a scholarship from UCLA." He would have been one year behind Kareem Abdul-Jabbar and one ahead of Sidney Wicks. But when the Yankees called, Ron answered.

"When they chose me as the first pick in the whole draft, it was a chance for this Jewish boy from Atlanta to go up north," Ron says. "Mantle had always been my hero." The four years he might have spent at Westwood was instead spent touring the Yankees' minor-league system. He came up to stay in June 1971. By his seventh game his batting average was over .300, and it fell below that level for only one game the rest of the season. He finished at .322. It looked like we had a good new bat for a long time. In fact, it seemed like he always had a bat in his hand—in the dugout, in the locker room, everywhere. For all I know, he carried one around at home.

Ron was always a fun guy, but not everybody enjoyed his many and diverse skills. Eating, for instance. "There was a place in Fort Lauderdale called Chateau Madrid. A lot of players went there during spring training. They had an all-you-could-eat special for maybe nine dollars. It's hard to believe now, but nine dollars seemed like a lot of money to most of us back then. It was a whole day's meal money," Ron remembers. "They had a 72-ounce steak on the menu with an open challenge. If you could finish the steak, you didn't have to pay for it."

Now, Ronnie's big claim to fame, other than his swing, was that he could outeat anybody. I think he won the steak challenge three times before they banned him from ordering it. A 72-ounce steak was no problem for him. It was like the blackjack tables in Las Vegas. If they know you can count cards, they don't let you play.

Of my relationship with Ron, he says, "Roy and I were teammates for eight years. He was a silent leader. I lived in Riverdale, New Jersey, not far from Roy. We did a lot of things together, in season and out. It wasn't like today, when everybody goes their separate ways after the game."

One of the things we did for many off-seasons was play basketball. We played benefit games against high school faculties.

Chris Chambliss played, along with Walt "No Neck" Williams, Thurman Munson, Gene "Stick" Michael, and Elston Howard. Elston was a lot older, but he was still a great athlete. There is a photograph of Elston from about 1964, jumping up at the plate to flag down a high throw. He looks about three feet in the air, and he's 35 years old and wearing full catcher's gear!

I think Stick was the best player. He played varsity basketball at Kent State and could dribble between his legs, pass behind his back, and everything. I think he could have played in the NBA. We also had some Mets playing, such as John Milner, Jon Matlack, and Ed Kranepool. Jeff Torborg, who was born and lived in New Jersey, played, too.

"These were friendly games. A lot of 30' jumpers, no banging under the boards," Ron says. "Oh, if I got a breakaway I might dunk once or twice. No Neck and Milner were the big scorers. And, no, Roy could not jump." He does add, however, when pressed, that I could, in fact, play.

"Today, they don't have games like this," Ron states, and he believes the players and fans are the poorer for it. "The players are making too much money to risk injuries. The teams won't allow it. Back then, we got a few bucks for the games and were happy to have the extra money. People forget how little ballplayers made back then, unless you were one of the few big stars. If they had games like that today, the stands would be full, just with the players' entourages."

Unfortunately, though he played a lot of winter hoops, he didn't get to play baseball nearly as much as he would have liked. He had several shoulder injuries, and his knees weren't all that good, either. I remember all too well the day he lost a battle to a fence in Winter Haven, Florida.

I was playing center and Ron was in left, in a spring-training game at the Red Sox's field. Yastrzemski sliced one down the line. We were playing Yaz like everybody did, way over to right, expecting him to pull the ball. Ronnie had a full head of steam and a long way to run. I yelled at him to pull up, to give up on the ball, but he never heard me.

The park in Winter Haven, like a lot of spring-training sites in those days, was not up to major-league specifications. This one had a very narrow warning track and no padding on the walls. He went for that ball at full speed. His shoulder and knee hit the wall at the same time. He was never the same after that.

"I had played exactly four games in left field before Billy Martin put me out there as a spring-training experiment," Ron says. "I hit that wall like a steamer hitting the Statue of Liberty. It was solid concrete; it did not move. I had just had rotator-cuff surgery. I had four knee operations after that collision, and they were not scopes like you have today. Every one of them took a long time to heal."

Arthroscopic surgery doesn't have to cut muscle to repair ligaments and tendons. When Ron was losing bouts to concrete walls, it was the healing of the muscles that kept guys out of the lineups so long. I was lucky I never had anything worse than hamstring pulls.

"Later I heard the county had to shut down that stadium," Ron says. "They lost a big lawsuit. Some kid hit the wall and got hurt like I did."

In fact, it was Ron's ability to get hurt seriously and often that led to his primary role in baseball history as the first designated hitter, in 1973. It must be noted that the first designated hitter didn't hit; he walked, off Luis Tiant.

"I wasn't conditioned to be a DH," Ron says. "Nobody was. To me, it was like pinch-hitting four or five times a game. But I had never pinch-hit very much. I sat on the bench between Elston Howard and Dick Howser and just tried to keep my head in the game. I began the season recovering from a hamstring injury, and that was a way to keep my bat in the game. It was hard, but I adjusted to it." Ironically, the record shows that the guy who was the first DH hit much better when he was also playing in the field.

I know what he means. I DHed in more than 100 games and didn't hit quite as well as when I was also in the field. I didn't like it. It felt like you weren't really in the game. If you didn't get any hits, it felt like you weren't helping the team to win. If you were in the field, you might go hitless but still help the team with a good catch, keep a ball from going to the wall, or hit the cutoff man.

It was difficult to stay loose, to go up to the plate after sitting on the bench for so long. We didn't know how to prepare to be designated hitters those first years after the rules allowed it. Now the DHs do a lot between at-bats, and the teams have a lot for them to do. They have batting cages close to the clubhouses, underneath the stands. You can take swings off a tee or soft-toss with a coach. There is video to study your swing or the pitcher's motion. Back then, I just tried to stay loose enough not to pull a muscle digging for first after sitting for a half hour or more. Now, guys play practically their whole careers at DH, and the game has changed, so they know what to do. There are a lot of ways the game has changed that fans don't see.

Ron started 1973 at DH but played a lot of first, too. What he mostly did that year was hit the ball hard. He ended at a career-high .329, but he was hot as Ty Cobb for a good part of the season. As late as the final week of June he was hitting .410! He also hit a rare trifecta, making the covers of *Sports Illustrated*, *Sport*, and *The Sporting News*.

This attention led to a most unusual invitation. Moshe Dayan and Golda Meir invited him to Israel. He didn't go, because of all the turmoil at the time. In 2007 there was still plenty of turmoil, but Ron didn't want to miss the chance to go under very unusual and compelling circumstances. He was named one of the managers in the brand-new Israel Professional Baseball League.

"I decided it was time for me to go," Ron says. "Art Shamsky and Ken Holtzman were managers, too. My team played on a kibbutz outside Tel Aviv, which had a lot of American expatriates, many from New York and New Jersey. They were Yankees fans! I loved it. The fans loved it. We filled our park every night."

The game was the same, except for one rule difference that probably gives baseball traditionalists the hives. "There were no extra innings. If the game was tied after seven innings, it was decided with a Home Run Derby," Ron says. "Each manager picked three hitters, and your coach threw to your hitters. Three swings each. Most over the fence wins. It was fun." Probably saved a lot of money on relief pitchers, too, not to mention the length of games.

Not every team was as successful as Ron's, because the game was completely new to some areas. Neither was there the financing nor overall coordination for a completely successful operation. But let the record state that manager Ron Blomberg won the pennant! His team wore Yankees blue pinstripes, and the logo on the cap was similar to ours, given that the letters were Hebrew. Even sweeter, he beat Art Shamsky's team 3–0 in the championship game after going 29–12 during the season. Art's team wore Mets colors.

"Yes, the Israel Yankees beat the Israel Mets!" Ron says with glee. "I beat Shamsky! Yankees over Mets. Yankees never lose." Ron tells of his victory with all the enthusiasm of that high school legend he was back in the 1960s.

Ron played his last major-league game when he was 30. As his managing experience has showed, he still has a lot of baseball in him, but his body surrendered long, long ago. He so enjoyed his time as a Yankee, abbreviated as it was. The money wasn't as good, but, like most of us, he believes the game was better, and, for sure, we enjoyed it more. "When I retired, Lloyd's of London wouldn't insure me anymore. I was having cortisone injections every three or four days. As far as my knees and shoulder, there wasn't anything left for them to fix," Ron recalls. "I know it sounds like I played back in the days of Abner Doubleday or somebody, but it really is a lot different today. But we had a ball."

The Arm Bone's Connected to the Leg Bone

If you can run and also have a little power, you probably will pull a hamstring sooner or later. If you're *real* fast and have a *lot* of power, like the Jacksons named Bo and Reggie, you are in danger of a hammy with every step you take. If you pull it once, the chances of pulling it again must be something like 99.9 percent. And again. And again.

Hamstring pulls were the only injuries I ever had, but they were enough. I had six official hamstring pulls and about a thousand almosts, not quites, and I wonders. They happen when you try to run faster than you can run. Trying to beat out a grounder to short with two outs and the winning run chugging down from third. Running into the left center-field gap, knowing that Mantle can't catch that ball anymore, with the bases loaded.

There's a pop and then 15 days on the disabled list. Maybe 30; who knows? The problem is, no doctor ever takes a stamp that says *healed* and applies it to your leg. It was tough for me, because speed was such a big part of my game. If Boog Powell or Frank Howard pulled a hamstring, how would you know? They'd miss two or three games and be back hitting big flies and waltzing around first base on defense. It didn't matter how muscular their legs were, they didn't run fast enough to pull a little red wagon, let alone a hamstring.

You can get your hitter's timing back by working in the cage for a few days before you come back. It's not the same as a game, but almost. What is tough is testing the leg itself, especially when you first return. You consciously have to tell yourself *not* to try to beat out a grounder to short or stretch a single into a double. In other words, you have to try to *not* do the very things that make you a good player.

If you hit a ball into the hole, you just continue to run at normal speed; don't downshift. Sometimes you get thrown out by a step, and you *know* you should have beaten it out. That's almost as frustrating as sitting on the bench waiting for it to heal. So, if you see a player who appears not to be going all-out in the outfield or on the bases, he may not be dogging it. He may, in fact, be a gamer who is coming back from an injury, trying very hard to contribute before he is 100 percent.

A hamstring pull feels like a knife being plunged into your leg. It's not a fun injury. Even so, it's not as bad as pulling an Achilles tendon. It used to be that if you snapped one of those, you were finished.

Surgery has improved tremendously since I played. Lasers and other technology have enabled recoveries that are far quicker and more complete than they used to be. Mickey Mantle might have played five more years and broken Ruth's records if they'd had lasers in his day. Also, with today's long-term contracts, a player with a severely pulled hamstring can sit as long as he needs without fear of losing his job. A lot of guys are out a year now, sometimes more, then come back strong. It never happened in the old days, because everybody, even the big stars, would be afraid to be out that long. There are a lot of reasons players last longer today.

Pitchers pull hamstrings, too. In 2007 Yankees pitching phenom Phil Hughes pulled one early in the season, and it was a long time before the Yankees let him touch a ball. They weren't going to risk a golden arm for a few extra starts. The Tigers did the same with Andrew Miller, their rookie southpaw and former No. 1 draft choice. They shut him down completely, even though they were still in the pennant race.

It wasn't always like that. Ask Fritz Peterson, one of the best Yankees pitchers in the post–Whitey Ford, pre–Ron Guidry era. "I won 20 games in 1970, but I didn't pitch any better or any worse than in several other years," Fritz insists. "What was better was our bullpen."

Lindy McDaniel and Jack Aker combined for 45 saves. "By 1970 you could sense the team getting good again. I won my 20th on the last game of the season," Peterson says. "It was Stan Bahnsen's turn, but Ralph Houk started me. He always let his starters get a chance at 20 if he could. Houk was like a father to me and a lot of other players. It was sad when he left. He knew how to treat players fairly."

Peterson continued to pitch well until he pulled a groin muscle in 1973. He missed a few starts, then assumed it was safe for him to start throwing again. It took a while for him to realize this was a big mistake. "I threw differently," he says. "I didn't know it at first, but I began to notice that the sides of my shoes were wearing differently than before." He had subtly changed his motion to compensate for the leg pain.

Dizzy Dean did a similar thing in 1937, when he was only 27, cutting his career so short it lasted barely long enough to qualify him for the Hall of Fame. Ole Diz was hit in the toe by a line drive off the bat of Indians outfielder Earl Averill in the All-Star Game. Diz was a tough Arkansas farmboy, an extreme competitor, and stubborn as a Missouri mule, to boot. Nobody could tell him to rest longer than he wanted, not with his St. Louis Cardinals in a pennant race. He was soon back on the mound. Far too soon, as it turned out. Like Peterson, Dean unconsciously altered his delivery and found his fastball was consigned to history. Traded the following April to the Cubs, he struggled several years, getting by on guile, guts, and changing speeds, but the real Dizzy Dean was gone. The broken toe might as well have been a broken arm.

One thing Dizzy didn't have that Fritz did was cortisone. Fritz took his first cortisone shot in 1973, shortly after he discovered that his arm hurt, as a result of the groin pull and altering his delivery. Today he might have taken long enough on the disabled list to heal completely, but nobody did that in the 1970s. "There were no long contracts back then. No one was sitting for a month waiting to heal," Fritz remembers. Teams had little invested in players, so they had little incentive to wait. They would just find a replacement.

Cortisone was new to baseball then. Not everybody was sold on it, and nobody knew for sure the effects, even in the short term, let alone the long. Naturally, the Yankees were conservative in this area, like they are in most everything. "The Yankees team doctor didn't believe in cortisone," Fritz says. "I had to go outside the organization to a private doctor."

Shortly thereafter Fritz was getting two cortisone shots a week. It kept him in the rotation but didn't allow him to recover his former effectiveness. The next year he was traded to the Cleveland Indians, but 1974 was another miserable season for him. The 1975 season brought a turnaround, a 14–8 season, but his winning percentage was deceptive. He started only 25 games and pitched 100 innings fewer than he did in his good years with New York. Even this level of effectiveness was bought only with more frequent shots.

At one time it was thought, at least by ordinary folks like baseball players, that cortisone helped in the healing process. It does, in as much as it takes away the pain. But healing happens only if you rest. However, with the pain gone, the athlete is tempted to play again. The price is that not only does the injury not heal, but it gets worse. Although an occasional cortisone shot can help a player get back in the game, continued use has ended a lot of careers or at least not fulfilled the hopes of extending them.

His last two years in the major leagues, Fritz Peterson took 150 cortisone shots.

In the winter, Peterson's friend, John Ellis, said that he could get Fritz traded to his Texas Rangers, and they could have fun. *Fun* was the name of Ellis' game, in addition to being a catcher–first baseman. He had played with Peterson in the minors and with the Yankees and Cleveland. Ellis was traded to Cleveland a year before Fritz, for a player who was maybe not as much fun but was a bit more of a factor on the field: Graig Nettles.

If there was little pressure to win in Cleveland, there was even less in Texas, which had never known a winner, except decades ago in the Texas League when Dallas was a Detroit farm team and young Hank Greenberg was first flexing his muscles. Texas wasn't much fun for Peterson, even with John Ellis. He started one game and relieved in two, and then came the game he will never forget, and not only because it was June 19, 1976, and Peterson's uniform number was always 19.

"I started against Baltimore and went six innings. I only gave up two runs, one earned. But I walked five and blew my arm out," Fritz recalls. He had led the American League in fewest walks per inning for five consecutive years, 1968 to 1972. Five walks in those days should have taken about 40 innings, not six.

"It was like it went dead. I didn't feel a thing that night," he says. "Two days later it was like a carving knife had been stuck in there. The doctor found a hole in my rotator cuff the size of a quarter. I had an operation but only got back 50 percent movement. Texas released me."

In the spring of 1977, he called Bill Veeck, who was in one of his several stints of owning the White Sox. Veeck was known as a good guy who would give a player a chance when nobody else would. Additionally, his new manager was Bob Lemon, who was Veeck's pitching ace in the 1950s when Cleveland had a great team.

Lemon was another good guy. His placid nature was essential when he came to the Yankees in 1978 and we won it all. Not many managers make a big difference. He did.

He was also more fun than even John Ellis. Herb Score, long-time Cleveland announcer and former Indians teammate of Lemon's, once told Peterson, "He's spilled more booze than you've drunk. His goal is to be the bartender of a bar in Hawaii where he is the only customer."

"Veeck spoke with Lemon, and Bill offered me a contract for more than I asked," Fritz says. "Veeck told me, 'Let's see if you can do it.'"

"What I did was blow out my arm again, in spring training. I was through now and knew it." Fritz points out, "It wasn't scary this time, even though I had just gone through a divorce and had a lot of financial and family problems. I had just found my belief in God, and that got me through."

Trading a belief in God for a belief in cortisone is a definite upgrade. Whether you are a pitcher or a position player, the leg bone's connected to the arm bone. The muscles, ligaments, and tendons that enable an athlete to perform can turn on him at any moment. I was fortunate that the various pulls I suffered did not keep me from playing 1,881 regular-season games. I rested enough, I guess, and was careful when I needed to be. A lot of guys were not so lucky.

Trades Are Part of the Game

"Trades are part of the game," everybody says. But they never were for me. I spent my entire major-league career as a Yankee, though this was as much my doing as the Yankees'. If they ever tried to trade me earlier in my career, I never knew about it, and they obviously never succeeded. When they wanted to, in 1978, I

Chris Chambliss, who was traded to the Yankees from the Cleveland Indians in 1974, became one of the main components that facilitated the Yankees' World Series championships in 1977 and 1978.

already had my 10 years in with the same team, which meant that they needed my permission, which I denied.

I was never one of Billy Martin's favorites, nor he mine. But then again, that wasn't unusual in those days, and, regardless of personalities, we won. I think, given the results, that I might have done Billy a favor when I refused to go to Oakland, as he almost certainly would have preferred early in the season.

After we were all but given up for dead in August, we came back to beat Boston on Bucky Dent's famous home run. Thanks to my preference to stay put, the .342 I hit that September was for the Yankees, not the A's. I also hit a homer in the final playoff game against Kansas City in the sixth inning to give my buddy Ron Guidry a 2–1 win over Dennis Leonard, clinching the pennant. I hit

.333 with another homer in the World Series. Maybe whomever Billy wanted in Oakland might have helped him more than I did, but I believe I was a good example of the old baseball chestnut, "Sometimes the best trades are the ones you don't make."

Of course, if Babe Ruth and Hank Aaron could be traded, it is no disgrace. Although you hate to see friends traded away, new ones are also made because of trades. One of my best friends in baseball is Chris Chambliss, who was traded to New York from Cleveland in 1974 and became one of the important building blocks of the championship teams a few years later.

"I was drafted by Cincinnati right after high school but went to college instead," Chris explains. "We had a great baseball team at UCLA. We lost in the College World Series to USC for two years, then won it my senior year, beating Arizona State in the finals, 2–1. I was pretty successful playing in Alaska after the college season was over, so I dropped out of school and sent letters to every team, telling them of my intention to turn pro. This was still before players had agents."

Cleveland and San Diego were tied with the worst record. San Diego was Chris' hometown. But it was the American League's year to pick first. Chris was the No. 1 draft choice in the country, and be became an Indian.

Like the Yankees when I first came to the majors, the Indians were not very good, so Chris, like me, appeared in the majors before he was fully prepared. People always looked at Chris, a big, strong guy, and saw home runs. Because he was rushed through the Cleveland farm system with almost no instruction, nobody had bothered to show him *how* to hit home runs.

That is, no one showed him how to pull the ball into the seats. And yes, it is something that can be, and is, taught, though not everyone can do it.

"It was always, 'Hit for power, hit for power,' but nobody taught me how. It isn't all about strength," Chris remembers. "Yes, I got stronger over the years, but I also got smarter or at least more experienced. It was more about learning *how* to hit home runs. Finding the pitch you can turn on. Being selective.

Fouling off or taking a pitch you might dump into the opposite field for a single."

It didn't happen overnight. In his first three years with Cleveland, he averaged fewer than nine homers, a small total for a big guy and former No. 1 draft choice. Meanwhile, Gabe Paul, the general manager who signed him out of UCLA, had gone to the Yankees. Paul had already acquired two of his favorite Indians—Sam McDowell, who was near the end of a career that had not fulfilled expectations, and Graig Nettles, who, like Chambliss, was a promising youngster. Gabe got his first baseman plus a decent starter and reliever for four pitchers early in 1974.

His first two years with the Yankees were similar to his Cleveland years. Then, on three straight pennant winners, Chris averaged 15 homers and 92 RBIs, not counting one of the most famous playoff homers in Yankees history—off the Royals' Mark Littell, which won the 1976 pennant.

It takes two sides to make a trade, naturally, and the pitchers that went to Cleveland included Fred Beene and Fritz Peterson. Beenie was a little right-hander who was almost unhittable in the few chances he got to pitch in 1973. Just as people expected Chambliss to hit homers because of his large size, people expected Fred to be cuffed around because of his small size. It didn't happen, but this was before the days of "Moneyball," when compiling good stats didn't guarantee you a place on the roster, especially if you were a 5'9" pitcher. Even Ron Guidry had a hard time convincing front-office people who had never tried to hit against him that he was a big leaguer, and he was way bigger than Beene. So Fred was easy trade fodder, even if he was far more appreciated by his teammates than he was by his bosses.

Fritz Peterson was another story. He had been in our starting rotation since 1966, replacing the sore-armed Jim Bouton. He had great control and won 20 in 1970, the one year the bullpen really helped him. Then in 1973 he was part of one of the most unusual stories in baseball history. He and teammate Mike Kekich swapped families. You probably heard of it if you were around at the time, even if you weren't a baseball fan. They swapped wives, children, houses, even dogs. The amount of public scrutiny this elicited surprised everybody on the team and in the front office.

When Fritz was traded, many people assumed it was because he had sullied the Yankees' image. This may have been part of it, but there was a more fundamental baseball reason. He had a sore arm. If Fritz were throwing with the same success of previous years, I'm betting the Yankees' sense of moral outrage would have been replaced by compassion, understanding, and tolerance combined with, by the way, the desire to win.

"I started taking cortisone shots in 1973, two a week, sometimes more," Fritz recounts. His first bad year was 1973. He was only 8–15, after years of being one of our most dependable arms. "I wasn't in the starting rotation in the spring of '74. I was wearing out. I expected a trade. I went to Gabe Paul and said something like, 'I won't go to Cleveland or Philadelphia.'" But he was in no position to demand that he not be sent to either of what were, at the time, baseball Siberias.

Peterson told McDowell and Nettles what he had demanded of Paul. They asked Fritz which side of Cleveland he wanted to live on, the east side or the west.

Sure enough, a few days later Fritz was in Cleveland, and the Yankees had a big first baseman who couldn't yet pull the ball but who would learn and become a great friend in the process.

Peterson found the change not exactly to his liking. "It was strange. It was almost like playing amateur ball back when I was a kid. There was no great pressure to win. The first time I faced the Yankees, I felt they were pulling for me, even though they wanted to win."

Fritz has a final, lasting memory of the sentimentality, or lack of same, in the big leagues. "When I left the Yankees, I asked the clubhouse guy, Pete Sheehy, who had been at the job since before Babe Ruth or something, to not give my No. 19 out right away," Fritz says. "The next game, there he was, Dick Tidrow, one of the guys I was traded for, wearing my old No. 19."

chapter 10
The Virdon Virtues

Bill Virdon tries on his new uniform at a press conference after being named the New York Yankees' new manager on January 3, 1974. With their new boss are Whitey Ford (left) and Yankees coach Elston Howard.

The Guillotine Squad

Yankees manager Bill Virdon had a well-deserved reputation for being laid-back. But that doesn't mean he was slow. In 1962 he won a Gold Glove along with two other outfielders named Clemente and Mays. In fact, occasionally he was a little too quick for me.

In 1974 I was nursing one of my frequent hamstring pulls. Some days I just couldn't run hard enough to play outfield but wasn't hurt badly enough for the disabled list. On those days Lou Piniella played left, and I joined an involuntarily hearty crew that called itself "the Guillotine Squad." You know, like a guillotine, Virdon's blade fell quickly.

Depending on the opposing pitcher and the state of my hamstring, the Guillotine Squad was likely to be, in addition to myself, Walt Williams, Chris Chambliss, or Mike Hegan. That is, we might be called upon to pinch-hit at a moment's notice. Most managers will give you a little warning, like, "Hey, Roy, stay loose. You might hit in the pitcher's spot next inning." Virdon, a man of few words, did not waste words with any such advance notices. He later managed the Houston Astros, but he should have managed them back when they were called the Colt .45s. He was a fast draw.

Fellow member Chris Chambliss remembers, "I think it was Walt Williams that thought up the name, or maybe he brought it with him from another team. But it fit us well. It was kind of hard to figure out when you might have to hit, especially if the game was out of hand."

The Guillotine Squad's worst nightmare was sitting on the bench for eight innings and then going up against Nolan Ryan when he had already struck out about a dozen. It would be two 100-mile-an-hour fastballs and then, just when you might have cranked up enough to make contact with the next one, here comes that big curve, starting out at your forehead and ending up at your knees. It was unfair.

Usually the squad members suffered less spectacularly, if no less acutely. Baseball is an exciting game, but that doesn't mean every game is exciting or even keeps you awake. When you are playing in Shea Stadium with about 9,000 people scattered in the stands, it feels like a private party. We were playing the White Sox, who that year scaled the very pinnacle of mediocrity, finishing 80–80. The pitching matchups were Mel Stottlemyre and Stan Bahnsen, two good pitchers but guys who won with little breaking pitches and guile, rather than eye-popping speed or knee-buckling curves.

Thanks to a small rally highlighted by a Ron Blomberg triple, we led 2–0 after one. That hit enabled Ron to tie his all-time record for triples in a season, which is two. An infield error scored a run for the Sox in the seventh, but nothing much else happened except lots of grounders.

With two outs in the ninth and Sparky Lyle in for Mel, Eddie Leon hit a bloop double down the right-field line. It was the utility infielder's only extra-base hit of the year, in which he hit all of .109. It is to Leon's credit that he somehow managed to get into 31 games that year.

So after two and a half hours, Virdon said, "White, you're hitting." I tried to act like I had been sitting since early evening, just waiting for his command, but I'm afraid my act wasn't very good. I tried to get loose as quickly as I could, while the rest of the Guillotine Squad tried to hide their collective sighs of relief.

I'd hit Bahnsen pretty well since he left the Yankees a few years ago. His strikeout total had diminished each year. But his head got smarter as his arm got slower, and he could still win. And frustrate the hell out of you.

It took only a few minutes for me to give my old friend Stan a special gift: his only strikeout of the game. As I walked back to the dugout, my head hung low in the accepted style, the Guillotine Squad members were chewing on towels or throwing them over their heads to hide the laughter that comes with the relief that it has been someone else, not you, who has been the victim of Virdon's sudden move. But we never knew who might be next.

That same feeling of being led to the guillotine doesn't require Bill Virdon, of course. It is a common feeling for rookies, the first times they feel themselves truly overmatched. Poor Chase Wright, a Yankees rookie making only his second major-league start in 2007, found his head not only chopped off but being paraded around Fenway Park on a pike after he yielded homers to four consecutives batters.

My buddy Lou Piniella promised to handle his outstanding young pitching prospect, Scott Kazmir, with kid gloves and not let him be embarrassed should things unravel for him during his rookie year with Tampa Bay in 2004. His first start began with five scoreless innings, and he must have felt that the big leagues weren't so hard. But in his second start, the A's scored three runs in the first inning, thanks to a stolen base, passed ball, outfield error, and a couple of singles. The blade fell before his protective manager could protect him very much.

A rookie feels pretty good about himself just getting to the big leagues, until he sees something he hasn't seen before and has no idea how to handle it. It isn't always Nolan Ryan's fastball and curve. For me it was Hoyt Wilhelm's knuckleball. The first time I faced it, I thought, *What in the hell is that? How are you supposed to hit that?*

I never did come up with the answer. I managed to make contact against him, sure, with the weakest little grounds and shallow flies you can imagine. I was 1-for-9 against him before he most graciously moved to the National League.

I had the same kind of luck in the All-Star Game. I made the team in 1969 and was feeling pretty good about myself. I was only 25 and in just my second season as a regular. It was in Washington back when the National League usually won. It was great being on the field with Mays, Frank Robinson, and a lot of other players I looked up to as a kid. I was one of the reserves, just hoping I'd get in the game. Finally I got called on to pinch-hit in the ninth inning.

Phil Niekro was pitching. He was the worst guy you can think of when you have just one shot at him. You want to face a conventional pitcher, not a knuckleballer!

Ball one, ball two. Having seen a couple, I then took two swings and fouled both. It got to 3-2. I fouled off a couple more.

Then I swung and missed. He threw a batting-practice fastball right down the middle! I got a great pitch to hit, or at least it normally would have been. But after swinging at his butterflies, his fastball looked like Nolan Ryan's.

I felt the same way the first time I faced Larry Sherry. He had been an ace reliever in the National League, and by 1966, my first full year, he was supposed to be over the hill. In the second game of the season I had gotten three walks and a double off Denny McLain, but he led 3–2. Sherry came on in the ninth inning. He struck out Mantle and got Richardson on a fly. Everybody told me, "He's got three pitches: a fastball, a change, and a really good slider. Watch out for the slider."

On the first pitch I saw the fastball. On the second pitch the change. On the third pitch I saw that supposedly really good slider. I saw it, all right. I didn't hit it, but I saw it. Game over. The first look you get at almost any pitcher can be tough. This would have been a little easier to take had I not also made the final out of the opening game, a 2–1 loss to Mickey Lolich. At least in that game I made contact. I popped to short.

Baseball is a frustrating game. Sometimes when you find yourself in a situation where you feel overmatched, it is a whole lot more than frustrating. The Guillotine Squad invented something that every big-leaguer needs: we found a way to laugh about it.

Emergency Replacement Therapy

A manager always has to be prepared, and Bill Virdon certainly was. He managed the Yankees for less than two years. In 1974 he was named Manager of the Year. Billy Martin replaced him in August 1975, but Virdon left a big impression on those he managed.

He started out as a Yankees center-field prospect in the early 1950s. There was another prospect, a few months younger, named Mantle. Virdon still proved valuable to New York, however. In 1954, before he played a major-league game, he was traded to the St. Louis Cardinals for Enos Slaughter, who helped the Yankees to three pennants as he played out his Hall of Fame career.

Even though Virdon was Rookie of the Year in 1955 for the Cardinals, he was traded again in 1956, this time to the Pittsburgh Pirates for two suspects. The mastermind of this trade was the Cardinals' general manager, Frank "Trader" Lane, who was let go when he suggested trading Stan Musial. He found refuge in Cleveland, where his memory lives in infamy for trading Norm Cash, Rocky Colavito, and Roger Maris.

Virdon found a home in the vast center field of Pittsburgh's Forbes Field. Perhaps playing next to high-profile personalities such as Roberto Clemente, Don Hoak, and Dick Groat helped Virdon to develop a personality that was low-key, to say the least, in keeping with his stolid Midwestern background.

He had managed the Pirates briefly before coming to us and represents the bridge between the many years that Ralph Houk managed the club and the volatile and successful Billy Martin times. He always sent his pitching coach, Whitey Ford, to the mound to talk to the pitchers. He sent a coach like Dick Howser out to meet with the umps before the games. He seldom argued with umpires or set foot on the field at all.

Needless to say, this was not what new owner George Steinbrenner was looking for in a manager. Virdon didn't leave because he failed on the field, but because he wasn't "Broadway" enough for George or something. Virdon went on to lead the Houston Astros for longer than any other manager in their history. Virdon's Missouri style suited Texas better than the Bronx. But his reticent style did not mean that he was unprepared, which I discovered one afternoon.

I jogged in from left field during a game and noticed a strange feeling in my pants. I was running a bit, ah, free and loose, shall we say. I tried not to look too strange while I ran into the dugout, where, as I suspected, my athletic supporter had snapped. That is, one of the elastic bands that attached to the waistband had blown out like a sprinter's ruptured hamstring.

Now, ballplayers prepare for every contingency. I have a dozen bats ready for every game. In my case, this meant a dozen different lengths and weights, since I change from week to week, sometimes from at-bat to at-bat. I also use a slightly heavier bat when I hit righty, my natural side. I have a spare glove and shoes. The equipment manager has extra socks, uniforms, and belts. It is not unusual for a player, especially a pitcher during the dog days, to change uniforms in midgame. But jocks? Nobody, it seems, had an extra jock. Who breaks a jock during a game? Apparently I was making baseball history.

Virdon might not have been known as a major baseball strategist, but that day he laid down the perfect sacrifice. While the other guys on the bench amused themselves at the rather tentative way I entered the dugout, we quickly discovered that there were no spare jocks anywhere to be found.

The manager motioned me to the runway. All the players knew what we were doing and predictably responded with a variety of catcalls they must have learned in their junior high locker rooms. When we returned, I was ready to take the field, secure once again. Virdon was swinging low and loose, but hey, he never left the dugout anyway, so who would know?

For weeks afterward, the main topic of conversation seemed to be that Virdon and I must be the "same size, ha ha." Neither of us could ever figure out who this was supposed to compliment and who it was supposed to insult. Though baseball leaves plenty of time for conversation, some things are best left unsaid. This was one instance where Virdon's silent style was golden.

Batting-Practice Magic

Bill Virdon had been a good athlete, for sure. When he managed the Yankees in 1974 and 1975, he was still in good shape and wanted you to know it. Like a lot of managers, he had some pet theories or workouts that he was convinced made a big difference. For

Bill Virdon practices for the St. Louis Cardinals at spring training in 1955. He had been a good athlete and carried much of that athleticism to the Yankees when he became manager in 1974.
Photo courtesy of Getty Images.

instance, he liked to throw special batting practice for hitters he thought were in slumps.

One of our bench players was a short, stubby outfielder named Walter Williams. He was 5'6" and at least 185 pounds. For better or worse, he is probably remembered best for his nickname: "No Neck."

This follows a long baseball tradition of players with nicknames based on a physical attribute. Given the nature of ballplayers and locker-room humor, these nicknames are almost never complimentary. Hal "Skinny" Brown. Bob "Fatty" Fothergill. "Stubby" Overmire. "Piano Legs" Hickman. "Hawk" Harrelson got his name from his face, not his outfielding ability.

George "Catfish" Metkovich wasn't named by Charlie Finley, as Jim "Catfish" Hunter was. If you saw a photo of George, you would see why he got his nickname. "Three Finger" Brown was the victim of a farming accident as a kid. His mangled fingers helped his breaking pitches. Even stars like Lou Gehrig were not immune. His teammates didn't call out across the dugout, "Hi, Pride of the Yankees," or "Yo, Iron Horse." They were more likely to say, "Hey, Biscuit Pants," an homage to the powerful first sacker's considerable hindquarters, the source of his extraordinary power. So Walter endured "No Neck" with some measure of good cheer, but I don't think he was all that thrilled with it, either. I just called him Walt.

Walt was having a rough time, not hitting his pitch. Virdon pulled him aside and said, "Walter, you need to come out for extra hitting. You hit the fastball pretty well, but they throw you a breaking ball and you don't have a chance."

So Virdon and Williams came out early, maybe 4:00 PM before a night game. Virdon started throwing, and Walt was killing the ball: line drive to left center, right center, a couple over the wall. He was feeling pretty good about himself, so he said, "Skip, spin me a few."

We all knew that Virdon's curve wasn't too impressive, a dinky little thing. Sure enough, Walter started hitting weak grounders and pop-ups. Virdon just looked in at him and didn't say a thing, but his silence said "I told you so" louder than any words. It did get Williams' attention. He put more concentration into hitting curves, and it helped him.

Once Virdon got me on the same thing. After a game he said, "Your swing hasn't been looking that good. Your stance is good, your start looks good, but when your bat gets to the point of contact, nothing happens." *Don't sugarcoat it, Skip*, I was thinking. But I said, "Which way, left-handed or right?"

"Both," he said.

So he took me out and threw BP before a game. I got a bloop single in that game, and Virdon was convinced I was cured. I guess sometimes the magic is pretty subtle.

The Watercooler Waltz

As everyone who has ever played baseball at any level knows, it can be a frustrating game. On the big-league level, sometimes it can be overwhelmingly frustrating for dozens of reasons: the long season, the travel, the media, and, of course, the constant pressure to perform well with a lot of everyone's money on the line.

Professional baseball players exhibit an amazingly composed demeanor in the face of all this. It is big news when a player loses his temper on the field or in the dugout. Even the guys with reputations of having volatile personalities keep it together almost all the time. There are probably more arguments and explosions during the course of the average softball beer-league season than in the majors, for one very good reason: losing your temper in the show can be expensive in many ways.

Baseball history has a special niche for the hotheads, those who fit that special baseball term of endearment, *red ass*. On the Yankees, the young Mickey Mantle was known for exploding as he tried to deal with the pressure of replacing the great DiMaggio. During his rookie year of 1951, Mantle struck out five times in a row while the Yanks were losing a Memorial Day doubleheader to the Red Sox.

Longtime announcer Mel Allen later told the story of how, when Mickey kicked the watercooler several times after strikeout five, Casey Stengel gently reminded the young center fielder, "Son, that watercooler ain't strikin' you out."

By the time I arrived, Mantle was older and more composed. Those Yankees teams of the mid-'60s were hardly contenders, so perhaps not having to fight for a pennant every year might have mellowed him.

Years after I retired, this part of Yankees history was embodied by Paul O'Neill, who frequently bubbled over with abuse toward bats or batting helmets that failed to provide hits in key situations. As Chris Chambliss, a Yankees coach during Paul's playing days remembers, "Paul lost it about every other day. He's the only guy I ever saw who could go 4-for-4, make an out on his fifth trip at bat, and go berserk."

Ted Williams was another hitter who could get extremely agitated, no matter how good a year he was having. During his days with the Red Sox, he had mellowed enough to limit his emotional releases to a few ill-chosen hand gestures and the occasional expectoration, many of them inspired by his war with a few Boston sportswriters, whose Williams-oriented vitriol was constant. When he was younger and playing minor-league ball, he was more demonstrative.

During a brief stop in Minneapolis, when it was the top Boston minor-league team, he occasionally showed his lack of interest in defense by sitting down in the outfield or his disappointment with a bad day by tearing his locker apart. After popping up with the bases loaded, he drove his fist through a watercooler. He hit .366 with 43 homers that year, on his way to Cooperstown. Imagine the damage he could have done had he ever been in a real slump!

In my day, Lou Piniella was the master. One night in Cleveland, Lou was having a bad game. He disappeared into the clubhouse for a few moments, which wasn't unusual. The corridor between the dugout and clubhouse wasn't exactly appointed like the Ritz. It was plain concrete, illuminated with a row of bare bulbs that Lou saw as sitting ducks or perhaps as batting-practice fastballs. He took his bat and knocked out every light, setting an unusual kind of record for most hits in one game.

We discovered his feat after the game, when we tried to walk through the corridor and found utter darkness. But the darkness was not a mystery to us. We all knew that it was just another of Lou's tirades.

As accomplished as Lou was at showing his emotions as a player, his rage did not fully develop, nor did he not really touch the depth of baseball's frustration, until he became a manager. It was then that his creativity peaked with his invention of the base abuse: pulling an offending base from its mooring and tossing it as far as possible. If he did not invent it, he certainly perfected it. I'm sure Lou holds the major-league record in base-tossing, for frequency, if not for distance.

Sometimes the equipment fights back. In old Tiger Stadium, the bat racks in both dugouts were at the back of the benches and were horizontal to the ground. You stuck your bat in them and pulled them out. If a bat caused you to strike out or ground weakly to the shortstop on a pitch you should have pounded into the left-field corner, the tendency was to teach that bat a lesson by returning it to the bat rack with as much force as possible. This was a mistake.

The other end of the bat rack was simply the bare concrete dugout wall, which, when a bat was slammed into it, exhibited a simple law of physics. That is, it recoiled out again with a force equal to which it had been slammed. Many hitters over the years learned this the hard way, including usually mild-mannered Tigers star Al Kaline, who broke a finger when his slammed bat returned to him forcefully and unexpectedly.

In the history of baseball, however, I'm sure that no piece of equipment has taken as much abuse as the watercooler, a silent victim, waiting to endure the misplaced fury of the recently thwarted. But even a watercooler can sometimes defend itself, and even the usually even-tempered can sometimes be driven to desperation. For instance, the usually even-tempered me.

I was always known as a guy who was calm and serene, but I did have a temperamental side, which could show if things weren't going my way. One day, we were playing the White Sox in Comiskey Park. I was going through a rough spot and was maybe zero for my last 16 or 17 times at bat. Jim Kaat was pitching, and that would put me in a bad mood from the time I saw his name in the morning paper listed as the starter. If I'd had to face Jim Kaat every day, I would have soon found another line of work. There was just something about the angle of his pitches. I couldn't pick up the ball very well, and after he started that no-windup delivery that extended his career several years, it got even worse.

It was about the fifth inning, and we are one run ahead with a runner on third and no outs. I always prided myself on getting that run home, even against the toughest pitchers. It's like a free run batted in. So I hit a nice fly to right. As I was running to first I was thinking it was a sure sacrifice fly and we would lead by two.

I was running to first, and I saw the right fielder running in. I kept running, and he kept running. The darned Windy City was blowing my nice sacrifice fly toward the infield. By the time I got to first base the right fielder was camping under a very, very shallow fly, barely beyond the infield dirt. Nettles didn't even think of tagging. No RBI, just another out: 0-for-18.

As I ran back to the dugout, I noticed the watercooler, which was at the first-base side of the dugout. Somehow I became very angry at the watercooler for just sitting there. Didn't it realize I had just been robbed of an RBI?

Now, this might have been a minor altercation, had it not been for one development. I had been taking karate all winter and had gotten pretty serious about it. Yes, karate is one of those Eastern martial arts that are supposed to, among other things, increase one's serenity. Let's just say I hadn't mastered that lesson yet. I snapped. I hit that watercooler with four or five shots. In football the technique would have been called a forearm shiver, which I had perfected in high school as an undersized running back. Now, thanks to karate, these shivers were delivered with much more focus and strength than I would have delivered to high school linebackers.

I popped the watercooler in its midsection, if a watercooler can be said to have a midsection. Bang! Bang! Bang! It was very loud. Then it began to fight back, making some strange sounds of its own. That's when the pipes burst.

I was a victim of technological progress. When Mickey Mantle or Ted Williams attacked watercoolers back in the 1950s, they attacked vessels that were unchanged since the days of Ty Cobb. I wasn't so lucky.

This watercooler was connected to the stadium's plumbing system. The pipes behind the cooler burst, and water started squirting everywhere. Although this literally may have cooled me down, it made my temper hotter. I started wrestling with the watercooler, twisting and turning. The whole thing came off in my arms. Teammates were scattering wildly.

"Did we get wet?" Chambliss recalls. "Oh, yeah. It was a wonder Roy didn't break his arm. We were really surprised. We were used to Roy just coming back to the bench and sitting down. But he had been grounding out to second, it seemed, for about two weeks. You know, that same annoying ground ball."

There was a stairway to the clubhouse to the left of the dugout. I tossed the whole watercooler down the steps. The cooler died, but the exploding pipes lived on. Fortunately, a member of the ground crew came to our rescue and turned the water off, but not before I was soaking wet.

Meanwhile, our hitter had just made the last out of the inning; time for me to take the field soaking wet. It was not my finest hour.

Bill Virdon called me into his office after the game and said, in what was an outburst for the soft-spoken Missourian, "We can't have that anymore." Right.

The White Sox general manager, Roland Hemond, saw it all. He phoned down to the dugout later in the game with his review. He said it was the best dugout performance he had ever seen—but there would be a bill.

I never saw one and never asked. Maybe the Yankees took pity on a guy in a slump. Maybe Hemond finally decided the show was worth the price. It was my greatest display of temper in my career. At least I made it memorable.

Two months later we returned to Chicago. There was the watercooler; or, more precisely, there was a *new* watercooler. But this one was different. It had about five iron bolts sealing it in, making it virtually impossible for anyone to repeat my performance, barring not only a black belt in karate but also an acetylene torch.

Of course, this provided great conversational material for my teammates, and not only for the rest of the year. I *still* hear about it. I am constantly reminded that, holding the big metal container in my arms, with water squirting everywhere, it was as though I was waltzing with the watercooler.

But my teammates also noticed the force of my mighty karate blows. If they are ever in a fight, they want me on their side, they say. Especially if they are fighting a watercooler.

chapter 11
The Years of Winning Dangerously

Billy Martin (left) talks to newsmen in New York on August 2, 1975, after being named manager of the New York Yankees, replacing Bill Virdon.

New Gun in Town

Everybody knew that there was a new gun in town when Billy Martin took over from Bill Virdon as Yankees manager late in 1975. One way we knew was that Billy sported cowboy clothes just about every day: boots, hats, shirts with pearl snaps instead of buttons, and those little leather ties with silver on the ends and at the neck.

I also found out in other ways. In one of his first games, we were playing Oakland, I think. I led off, got on, and moved to second on a single. Lou Piniella was hitting. I looked down at Dick Howser, the third-base coach, and there was the bunt sign. No outs. I took my lead. Lou squared up and fouled it off. I really didn't look for a sign after that. I just figured Lou was still bunting. I didn't see anybody signal anything, or at least that's what I think.

Lou swung away and hit the next pitch into left field for a single, and I scored. I walked into the dugout, everybody was slapping my hand, and I was feeling pretty good about myself, when Billy came over to me and said, more or less confidentially, "Did you know you missed a sign?"

"What?" I asked.

"Yes," said Billy. "The hit-and-run was on."

Right then a light went on. "I gotta start really paying attention," I thought. Billy was going to be doing things that not only the other team didn't expect, but that *his* team didn't expect, like hit-and-running with two guys on, with the batter behind on the count. I thought I did great to score the run, and he said, "Nope, you missed a sign." He wasn't all that happy.

"Billy created tension on his teams," says Henry Hecht, baseball beat writer for the *New York Post* during Billy's time as manager. "That gave them an edge. His Yankees played very, very aggressively. It couldn't be sustained. But they never ran away from a challenge."

In 1976, Billy's first full year, I had the most fun in my career, because he had me hitting second. I got to do things at the plate

I liked to do, such as bunt, hit and run, and hit behind the runner. In previous years, I often had to hit in the middle of the lineup, third or fourth. I wasn't really a power guy. I always wanted to hit first or second. Of course, winning the pennant added to the fun of 1976, too, to say the least.

When he came to the Yankees Billy must have been the only guy in Manhattan wearing cowboy clothes, except for that guy in the Village People. But after getting to a couple of World Series, there were a lot of people who wanted to dress like Billy Martin. He opened a fancy, expensive western shop on Madison Avenue, next to some of the most fashionable stores in the world. It was so successful that one might argue that *Urban Cowboy*, the John Travolta movie that came out in 1980, was influenced by the new wave of urban cowboys tricked out in Billy Martin's boots, belts, shirts, hats, and other regalia.

Billy Martin Jr., who now lives in Arlington, Texas, and is an agent for baseball players, traces his dad's influential fashion sense to his years as manager of his hometown Texas Rangers, right before he came to New York. Billy's best friend, Mickey Mantle, lived in the area and turned him on to country-and-western music. The Texas atmosphere in general awakened in Billy a deep appreciation for all things western. "He read Louis L'Amour novels and also read a lot of Western, Native American, and Civil War history." Billy remembers. "He really felt he was a misplaced gunfighter."

Hall of Fame broadcaster Ernie Harwell suggests Billy's western mode existed, perhaps in nascent form, even before Texas. "Billy used to come over to my house during spring training when he managed the Tigers," Ernie says. "I lived next door to the novelist Erskine Caldwell, who was a huge fan. Every time Billy visited, Caldwell came over, and we talked baseball all night. Even then, Billy had a bit of a western fashion sense." Maybe it was the informality of spring training, maybe he let himself go in a Florida environment that was more accepting of western wear, but he wasn't wearing cowboy hats in Detroit during the season. He really didn't commit to the look until Texas.

The Manhattan store continued to do well, expanding at various times to additional outlets, including Los Angeles and the richest section of Long Island, the Hamptons. A catalog business followed. Although Billy and his family have not had a connection to the brand since 1982, it lives on. Billy Martin boots are established as one of the best and most upscale of all boots and are a special favorite of the rich and famous. Bob Dylan wore a Billy shirt on the cover of one of his CDs. Madonna wore a Billy belt on one of hers. When Arnold Schwarzenegger wed Maria Shriver, he personally selected sterling silver belt buckles from Billy's store for everyone in his wedding party. Billy Bob Thornton calls Billy's "his favorite store."

Strangely enough, there are now a lot of people who know the name Billy Martin as the brand of very cool, very expensive cowboy boots. To those people, I've got a news flash: he also used to manage some baseball teams.

A Triple-Threat Man

I don't know if the Yankees in the 1970s were the first team to stretch before games in an organized manner, but we were certainly one of the first. It was started by the players, mostly guys who had played football, like Chris Chambliss and me, and not by the coaches.

Chris played football, basketball, and baseball in high school around San Diego, California. He began at tight end because of his size but was moved to running back because of his speed. You're probably thinking, *Chris Chambliss, speed?*

"I was moved to the backfield after they found out how fast I could run. And I was a *big* running back for those days," Chris remembers. "The combination of size and speed earned me a football scholarship to junior college. I still played baseball, though. One day a scout from UCLA came by, and I hit six or seven out in a row. The next thing I knew, I was a UCLA baseball player, and I put the pads away."

No, Chris was not known for his speed in baseball. "I had good speed at first," Chris insists. "I beat out grounders to short in the minors. But I was never really coached on how to utilize my speed—how to get out of the box quickly or take secondary leads." A secondary lead is a walking lead, where a base runner is able to move an extra step or more toward the next base after a pitcher is committed to throwing home. It requires a rhythm and a feel for base running that even the fastest runners have to learn. Chris says, "If you don't look like you can run, they assume you can't and don't teach you."

Coaches took one look at Chris and imagined him hitting the ball over the fence, not going from first to third on a short single to right. After a few years, this became a self-fulfilling prophecy. He learned how to pull the ball into the seats and got slower year by year.

Part of the reason we stretched is the dreaded hamstring pull, which we ex–football players seemed to have more often than the rest. Hamstring injuries were the only thing that could keep me out of the lineup. Reggie Jackson suffered from them, too. So most of us stretched and ragged on each other while we stretched, just to make it interesting.

"I might say, 'You plan on making any contact tonight?'" Chambliss confesses. "We'd say that to anyone who struck out a few times the previous game. It was a way of keeping loose." But not everyone stretched.

Mick the Quick, for instance. Rivers sometimes wouldn't even come out for batting practice! He'd be in the players' lounge in his underwear. I'd say, "Hey, Mickey, you gonna take any swings?"

"No," he'd say. "I'm too tired." There was a little bumper-pool table in the clubhouse. He'd stay at that table until about 10 minutes before the game, practicing fancy shots. Then he'd put on his uniform, come out of the dugout, lead off, hit a line drive into the gap, and cruise into third standing up. We should all be so tired.

Then he'd come into the dugout and complain, "Man, my legs are really sore."

Then I said to Mickey, "If you stretched with us once in a while before the game, maybe you wouldn't walk like an old man by the sixth inning."

But Mickey never stretched, and so he was always sore as he sped around the bases. But that was Mickey. He was exactly the kind of player he wanted to be. He was a triple-threat man: run, hit, bumper pool.

Oscar

Oscar Gamble was smaller than I was, but he was considered a power hitter, especially by Oscar Gamble. When asked how he hit with runners in scoring position, he once said, "When I'm at bat, I'm in scoring position." He also played with and for some of the most colorful personalities in baseball history. His two stints with the Yankees helped, of course, but so did getting his ticket punched at several other stations.

He began in the majors as a teenager with the famous 1969 Cubs, who almost won the pennant, losing famously to the Miracle Mets. His manager was Leo Durocher, who, at age 64, was every bit as annoying in 1969 as he had been as shortstop for the Gashouse Gang in St. Louis 35 years earlier. "You could hear his voice all over the park, and he didn't exactly take you over to the side to say you had made a mistake. Everybody in the ballpark heard about it." Oscar says. "If you had a weakness, he'd let you know and everybody else know."

Durocher was a very aggressive manager. "He was fanatical about taking extended leads off bases," Oscar says. "You'd hear him yelling at you, 'Get up! Get up! Get up!' He wanted you as far off the base as you could get, which was usually so far that we were sure we would be picked off." If Leo made everybody uptight, another Cub helped everybody relax.

"Ernie Banks was a funny guy. He just said things in a humorous way. He didn't tell jokes or anything; more lighthearted, I guess you might say," Oscar remembers. "I was just 19 and came to the

Oscar Gamble leaps high beside Yankee Stadium's left-field wall on April 18, 1976, attempting to snatch a ninth-inning home run stroked by Minnesota Twin Butch Wynegar. When Gamble joined the Yankees, he was not given his uniform until he shortened his Afro.

big leagues from Double A." Oscar hit .298 for San Antonio and came north in June. "I had no idea how major leaguers were supposed to act. With the Cubs, of course, all our home games were during the day. It was tough to adjust after playing so many at night with any other team. Banks knocked on my door every day, made sure I got up on time. He showed me the right way to do things, what was expected of me." Ernie helped with the little things, which added up to the big thing of how to stay in the majors.

After 1969 Oscar was traded to Philadelphia, where he was a part-time outfielder who didn't show much power. Yet he credits another Hall of Famer with helping him develop some. Ironically, it was a pitcher. "Steve Carlton used to do all these strange little exercises to strengthen his hands and wrists. He'd always be squeezing rubber balls, little grippers. He did martial arts exercises, too. I began to use my whole body to hit. I bent down low to get all my strength behind my swing," Oscar says. "But getting my wrists and hands strong was the key. Power is all about bat speed, not strength."

By the time Oscar found a fairly regular job in the Cleveland Indians outfield, he was banging the ball out of the park on a regular basis. In 1975 he found himself with another legendary wrist-hitter, like Ernie Banks. He played on the Indians when Frank Robinson became the first black manager. It was also the year he let his famous Afro get as large as it ever got.

"The hair was just part of me," Oscar says. "I'd grow it longer in the off-season, then cut it in the spring, but one year I just didn't cut it. The Indians didn't care. Back then you tried to get away with as much as possible. We had Dave Duncan with the Indians for two years, too." Duncan, after serving in the National Guard, which required very short hair, let it hang below his shoulders once his hitch was up. A lot of the black guys had Afros of some length or another, "naturals," as they were called. I had one, but it didn't compare with Oscar's. Nobody's did. I had an obligation not to keep mine very long. It was Yankees team policy.

"Everybody wondered what would happen when my big Afro came to the Yankees," Oscar recalls. "I got to New York, and there was my locker, with my name on it and everything. Everything was in it but my uniform."

"Where's my uniform?" Oscar asked.

Billy Martin said, "George says you get it when you cut your hair."

Elston Howard took him to the barbershop. Oscar begged, "Please let me wait just a few days. I got an Afro Sheen commercial! They're gonna pay me to have it cut, like Namath was paid to cut his mustache. Please!"

"No dice. I had to get it cut right then." Oscar now admits, "Nobody knows, but right after, George found out how much I was going to be paid for the commercial and wrote me a check."

I had to play for the Yankees 11 years before we won a pennant. Oscar was 1-for-1, but after the 1976 season, he was gone again, traded to the White Sox in the deal that brought us Bucky Dent.

In Chicago he ran into two more Hall of Famers, owner Bill Veeck and manager Bob Lemon. The team won 90 games and finished third, higher than anyone predicted. It is a team, however, that is far better-known for its uniform than its record. It was the 1970s, and anybody who is so unfortunate to have photos from that decade will know what I mean. It was the day of big, wide, ugly ties; polyester suits with huge lapels; white zipper boots; huge Afros like Oscar's; and worse. But nobody wore anything that brought the house down more than the 1977 Chicago White Sox. This is the Major League Baseball team that wore shorts.

They did not wear them that often, but even once would have been too much. "Nobody wanted to wear them," Oscar sighs. "Other teams made fun of us, laughed at us. We sure as hell didn't want to slide. And it wasn't just the shorts. The shirts had big, floppy collars, like the old-time players'. And when we did wear long pants, we had these funny ones that were loose at the bottom, not bell-bottoms, but not like baseball pants, either. It was just too weird."

Veeck was an innovator and a chance-taker. Some of his chances paid off, like bringing African American players to the American League, and others, like shorts and his son Mike's Disco Demolition Night of a couple of years later, did not.

Oscar liked Veeck very much. "He came into the clubhouse a lot. The most of any owner I ever saw, by far. He was a very, very smart guy. Nobody on the team expected to do as well as we did. He was a fine motivator, a fine person," Oscar says. "He had to be a motivator and smart, because he didn't have much money. He put that team together for just that one year, but that's what he had to do every year."

Oscar had his best year with Veeck, hitting career highs with 31 homers and 83 RBIs. It was a good enough year that Veeck could no longer afford him. Oscar tried that new thing called free agency. He signed with San Diego and played about as much as he had in Chicago, but was about half as productive. In almost no time, he bounced through San Diego and Texas, finding his way back to the Yankees in 1979, the week Thurman Munson died. Not good timing.

Oscar's second Yankees tenure included the 1981 World Series and also the Steinbrenner manager-go-round, which, from 1979 through 1984, went: Lemon to Martin to Howser to Michael to Lemon to Michael to King to Martin to Berra. He finished his career in 1985, DHing and pinch-hitting for the White Sox and yet another Hall of Famer, Tony La Russa.

Everybody who played with Oscar will tell you what a great, upbeat guy he is. And he is certain of his place in history. "Hair and homers, that's what I'm famous for," Oscar says, "But more for the hair."

Outfield Robbery

Over the years, a lot of outfielders reached over the fence and robbed me of homers, but usually I got them back. I remember Frank Robinson fell completely into the stands to rob me. It took me several years, but I got him. The only guy I never got back was Paul Blair. He took away a three-run homer from me in Baltimore. He was so fancy about it; a photo of the catch was the main attraction in the sports section the next day!

A few days later what shows up in my mailbox? That photo of Blair showing off. Guess who it was from? Paul Blair! I know why. He thought he was getting even.

"We played against each other in high school," Paul says, now retired and still living in Baltimore. "I went to Manual Arts High, and he went to Centennial in Compton. His team beat mine for the championship, 4–3. I was getting back for that. We always had a friendly competition. We are the same kind of quiet guy."

Now, the fact is, Paul was a big high school star in Los Angeles. Back then, Compton was almost considered a suburb. We never even played Paul's team! So he thinks he's getting back at me for some game I didn't even play in. And it cost me a home run.

I was a second baseman back then, and Paul, as always, was center field. He tried to get the Dodgers to sign him right out of high school, but they said he was too small. He did sign with the Mets in 1961, a year before they really existed. "They sent me to Santa Barbara, and I had a good year. The Mets obviously didn't have a lot of players, so they promoted me to their Triple A roster," Paul remembers. This wasn't a good move for the new team. "There was a rule back then that a first-year player could get drafted by another team if the new team would put you in a higher league. So the Orioles drafted me and put me on their major-league roster. At age 20, I was in the majors at the end of the year. I had one at-bat, and so did another kid outfielder named Lou Piniella. The next year I was the regular center fielder."

If the Mets had kept Paul, he might have been in center field for them instead of the Orioles in the 1969 World Series. Tommie Agee got famous for a couple of amazing catches that fall. If Paul had been out there, you can be sure they would have been caught, too. He might have even made them look easy. He was the best center fielder during the time I played, one of the best of all time. He was able to play so shallow that he could catch lots of balls that fell in front of everyone else. Yet I never saw a catchable ball go over his head.

"I could play shallow because I had no fear," Paul says. "I could turn my back on the ball and not worry that I would lose it. I always played that way, and they let me do it. I played where I figured most of the balls would be hit."

I was happy to see Paul come to the Yankees for the 1977 and 1978 seasons. He had been an Orioles regular for a dozen years, yet he was willing to be a backup with us. Even though he didn't play every day, he definitely helped us win those two championships. It was good to see another quiet guy like me on the team. There weren't a whole lot of us.

"When I came to New York, Billy Martin made it easier for me to accept not being a regular. He said he needed me to come over with him and help him keep the peace," Paul recalls. "Players respected me. I kept guys like Rivers in good spirits and kept people away from Reggie. That stuff was only a problem before the game. During the game these guys were all pros. Billy played me all around the outfield and even the infield. I never played a major-league game at short or second until I was 34!"

Look on the rosters of World Series winners. More often than not you will find a guy like Paul, a veteran of previous winning teams who, as Yogi might say, can teach the other guys his experience.

"I'm more of a calm-type person," Paul says. "On the Yankees I could help with winning because of my time in Baltimore. I could help others understand what the goal is. Keep our eyes on winning the World Series." You would think everyone would focus on this all the time, but they don't. Just like in every business, people get obsessed with their individual goals; they get side-tracked by nonsense that goes on between people. Throw in a hundred writers and announcers asking questions, taking pictures, and printing your errors every day like in New York, and a few calming influences are important.

Paul said about me, "Roy was a big part of those Yankee teams, because he wasn't part of the turmoil. You must have some guys who are steady and can be counted on every day."

Thanks for the kind words, Paul, but no thanks for the photo of you taking a homer away from me. I guess if Reggie thought he was the straw that stirred the drink, maybe Paul and I were the twist of lemon: what you need to make the drink complete.

An Uplifting Experience

I don't have to think very long to recall my favorite baseball memory. It's a baseball going out of Yankee Stadium, hit by Chris Chambliss, to beat the Royals and put us in the World

Series. It's one among many famous Yankees homers, but it's No. 1 to me.

It was 11 years from the time I got my first major-league cup of coffee to my first pennant winner, not what anyone expected who began in the Yankees farm system in 1961, when the team was on top of the baseball world.

Little did I know that while I was making my way through the minors, the big club would be winning its last pennants for a decade. In the late '60s, when I was trying to establish myself as a big leaguer, I sometimes wondered if the team would ever contend again. CBS owned the team and didn't know enough about baseball to use its considerable resources wisely. Then George Steinbrenner bought the team. Say what you will about George, winning was No. 1, and he didn't give up.

That Kansas City Royals team was tough. We fought them evenly through the first four games. In the first inning, John Mayberry hit a two-run homer off Ed Figueroa. Then Dennis Leonard, in a rare bad start, gave it right back. I singled Mickey in after he led off the game with a triple. I stole second and scored on Chambliss' sacrifice fly.

Chris knocked me in again with a grounder, after I walked in the third, and we went ahead 4–3. We scratched out two more in the sixth, to which I contributed a sacrifice bunt, and our 6–3 lead looked pretty solid, except for one pitch to George Brett. As good as George was in the regular season, he ratcheted up even more for the postseason, especially against us. He put a Grant Jackson pitch out of the park with two on in the eighth to tie the game 6–6.

You could feel the breath go out of us on the Yankees bench. Brett just sort of deflated us. We had worked so hard. The ups and downs of the game repeated the longer pattern of the series and the even longer pattern of the entire season. *Oh, no, they tied it up*, we all thought. *Nuts.* Or words similar and perhaps a bit stronger.

There is no question that momentum is real in football and basketball. It is said that in baseball, momentum is as good as your next day's pitcher. But what about within a game? I think it takes something out of a team to see a lead that was established slowly over eight innings vanish with one swing of a bat. I know I felt that way.

I felt even more deflated after we went out in order in the bottom of the eighth. I made the second out. I hit the hell out of one, but it was on the ground, two hops to Mayberry playing deep on the grass.

Dick Tidrow pitched the ninth and was exactly as good as he needed to be. He got out of the inning by leaving two men on. Most important, he left Brett on deck. If he had gotten up with runners on—I don't want to think about it, even now.

Then, leading off the ninth against Mark Littell, Chris hit one hard, like I did. But he got under it, like I did not. From the dugout, we couldn't tell if it was going out. The outfielder had a bead on it. He was going to jump. He kind of disappeared for a second, and we didn't know right away. Then we did.

I started to run out on the field along with everybody else, not just from the dugout, but from the stands. I never made it beyond the on-deck circle. Four or five people lifted me in the air, which was not a happy place for me to be. As Chris was doing his Jim Brown imitation, knocking people down trying to find his way to home plate, I just wanted to get my feet on the ground again. It's a little scary, not a good feeling, to be lifted five or six feet off the ground, and you don't know who is doing the lifting.

When they let me down, I saw all those crazy people grabbing the bases. I fought my way back to the dugout, back to the clubhouse, and waited for the coast to clear. That game was the beginning of the end of fans going crazy after playoff games. I remember when the Phillies brought the mounted police out to protect the players and the field just a few years later. All that security on the field looked pretty strange and intimidating, but believe me, it was a lot less scary to me than being carried around the on-deck circle!

Watching Reggie Jackson's three homers in 1977 gave me goose bumps. It was just an amazing feat to witness. But I didn't play in that game, and it was never that close, so it didn't have the same drama for me. Bucky Dent's homer surprised me as much as anyone, and it certainly brought us home after an incredibly tough season. But for me, Chris' homer is my No. 1 memory, because for me it was reaching the top of a mountain after a very long, long climb.

chapter 12
After All Those Years

New York Yankees Reggie Jackson (left) and Bucky Dent smile happily in the locker room after their home runs defeated the Boston Red Sox 5–4 to win the American League pennant on October 2, 1978, at Fenway Park. Dent is responsible for a Roy White bat being in the Hall of Fame.

My Hall of Fame Bat

Tony Taylor was a good little second baseman for the Phillies for the entire decade of the 1960s. He played well into the 1970s as a useful part-time infielder, with a few years off in Detroit, where he helped the Tigers win the American League East in 1972. He never hit more than nine homers in a year. Most years he was more likely to park only three or four. Yet his bat hit four home runs in one game and is in the Hall of Fame in Cooperstown, New York.

His *bat* hit four home runs in a game, not Tony. Teammate Mike Schmidt hit four homers and drove in eight runs using one of Tony's bats. It was only the fifth game of the season in 1976, Tony's last year. He hadn't even gotten into a game yet. It was in Wrigley Field, and it was one of those games that seem to happen only in Wrigley. The Cubs led 12–1 at the end of three but managed to lose the game 18–16 in 10 innings.

Schmidt's hitting led the comeback, and for some reason he was using Tony's bat. It happens. I know, because my bat is in the Hall of Fame, too.

Some guys, like Thurman Munson, would use the same bat all year, every year. Then again, Thurman didn't change much from year to year about anything. I always wished I could be like that. Just settle into one bat that always felt comfortable to me. But, no, I kept changing bats all through my career. Maybe it was because I was a switch-hitter and felt a little stronger from the right side, my natural side. I used a little heavier bat hitting righty.

I was always checking other bats, looking for an edge. When I played in Japan for three years after I finished playing in the states in 1979, I noticed more variety to the bats there. Some of what they were doing in Japan 30 years ago has come over here now, just like some of the Japanese players. You see bats now where the end of the barrel is concave or, less frequently, where the end is almost sawed off flat. These styles came from Japan. It is thought that slightly less weight in the barrel allows for a lighter, and therefore quicker, swing. It is like corking a bat, only within the rules.

More recently, some American players have gone to bats with very large knobs. Placido Polanco, one of the leading hitters of the 2007 season, began the season with a bat with a very, very large knob. As the season wore on and his strength wore down, you could see the bat change. The knob got smaller and smaller.

Some players will wind several layers of tape around the knob, making it look like a billy club or some other weapon that might be useful if you found yourself cornered in an alley. The bigger knob is thought to create a lever affect, causing the barrel of the bat, again, to swing a little faster.

When I was in the minors, I not only switched bats all the time, but I switched stances, too. I think that went back to when I was a kid playing sock ball in Compton. I was Stan Musial and Stan Lopata, two power-hitters who both had really weird crouches. But I was also Nellie Fox and Dick Groat, two singles hitters who sprayed to all fields. The guy I ended up imitating for the longest time was Johnny Callison. He was a little bit older than I was and already established in the Phillies outfield. We were about the same size, and I could see that his stance generated a lot of power.

It was slightly open, with his hands held high, a little behind his ear. He went straight into the ball. I was the man of a thousand stances, but I always more or less came back to Johnny's. It was cool when, at the end of his career, he came to the Yankees. He had hurt his arm and couldn't throw anymore, but the stance was the same. He was a nice, soft-spoken guy, and I liked the way he carried himself on the field as well as at bat. I never mentioned that I had been influenced by his batting stance. I wonder now if he ever noticed.

When I was starting out, the other guys ragged me about my constant experimenting. "White, make up your mind for once, would ya?" I'd hear from Ian Dixon or Dave Turnbull. I must admit, at least once I took it too far.

We were playing the Tampa Tarpons, a farm club of the Cincinnati Reds. My first time up I got a little hit through the infield, but I didn't like the way it felt, so the next time up I used a different bat. Another hit, but I didn't really scorch the ball, so I changed again. My third time up I got another single with yet another bat. By this time I felt, "Hey, I'm 3-for-3 with three different bats; I better keep changing." Such is the logic of the professional baseball player.

By this time all the guys were saying, "Use my bat, use mine." So I did keep changing, and I had five hits in five times with five different bats! I didn't use five different stances, though. That would have been just too weird.

By the time I reached the majors, I was still changing bats more than most hitters, but my changing had become more purposeful. I knew I'd get weaker as the season wore on. I'd start out a season weighing 170, and that's what it usually said on the back of my baseball cards. But in fact, for most of the season I'd be less than that and would finish closer to 160. I'd be eating honey and protein shakes to keep up my strength, even as I was losing weight. Going to lighter and lighter bats helped, which is how a Roy White bat got into the Hall of Fame.

At batting practice before the famous playoff game of 1978, Bucky Dent was complaining about how bad his swing was. He hadn't been hitting. He swung a big bat that was called an MC44 model: big barrel, medium handle, 36" long, weighing 34 ounces. Then he choked way up, four or five inches. I had ordered a couple of dozen similar bats, except they were two inches shorter and two ounces lighter. For some reason, this particular batch never felt right in my hands. They were perfectly good bats, I just didn't like them, so I gave them to Mickey Rivers.

When Bucky complained about his swing, I suggested to him that he try one of the bats I gave to Rivers. "It's the same model as yours but shorter and lighter," I said. "Maybe you'll get around a little quicker, help your swing." Rivers gave Bucky one of the bats I had given him. Dent tried it out in batting practice, liked it, said it felt good, and decided to use it in the game.

Later, Bucky came up with Chris Chambliss on second, and I was on first. He fouled a ball off his ankle and called timeout. While the trainer was out spraying the cold stuff on Dent's ankle to dull the pain, Rivers noticed there was a chip off the knob of the bat Bucky was using.

"Why you using a chipped bat?" Rivers yelled out to him from the on-deck circle. "Use mine."

"I don't want to use your gamer," Bucky said. That is, he didn't want to ask Rivers for another bat, especially the one Rivers planned to use in his next at-bat, which happened to be the closest one available of that model.

"Hey, we're on the same team," Mickey said, giving his bat to Bucky, with every baseball fan in America watching. I knew immediately that Bucky's hit was going to be high off the wall, at least, but I couldn't tell if it would clear the wall. I ran as fast as I could in case Yaz missed the carom. Then I saw his head just drop, like he had been hit hard in the stomach. There was a sudden, vast silence. I knew it was gone.

Yes, it was Mickey Rivers' bat. But I gave it to Mickey, and it says *Roy White* on the barrel. And that's how my bat got into the Hall of Fame. I've gotta go see it someday.

Reggie, Too

Very rarely does a sportswriter get top billing over a superstar, but Henry Hecht did. Henry was a baseball writer for the *New York Post* from 1974 through 1983, the first eight of those years as a beat writer. For the first half of that stretch, he split the seasons between the Yankees and Mets, changing at the All-Star break. The switch was supposed to keep writers from getting too chummy with players or having them go stale or inattentive to circumstances that had become too familiar.

Whether it worked or not, Henry was a respected writer, known as a straight shooter who called it like he saw it from the press box and got his stories right in the clubhouse. This is important, because a writer who doesn't understand the game, bears grudges, or carries rumors can cause as much trouble for a team as an ace pitcher with a tear in his rotator cuff.

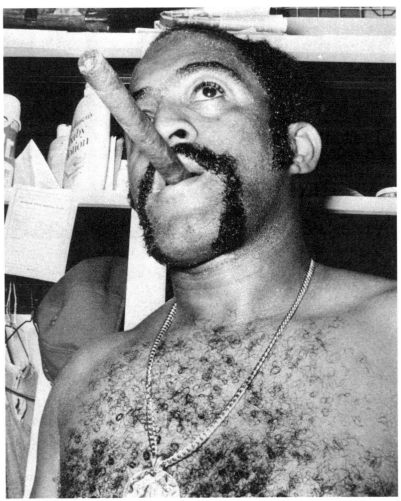

Luis Tiant, traded to the Yankees from the Red Sox in 1979, once gave Henry Hecht a demonstration of his ability to smoke a cigar in the shower without getting it wet.

If the fans of the 1960s and 1970s felt they knew Mickey Mantle or Reggie Jackson more than today's fans know A-Rod or Mariano, it is because writers used to spend far more time with the players, and in different circumstances. Once upon a time, writers and most players made something approaching the same salary, so they were more likely to frequent the same restaurants and watering holes. This began to change in the 1970s, even before the advent of free agency, but it was also before talk radio, ESPN, and the Internet, so there were far fewer media members crowding the clubhouse. Then, the beat writers often traveled with the team, stayed in the same hotels, and took the team bus to and from the park. All that has changed now. Although writers still get clubhouse time, it is more restricted and programmed, leaving fewer chances to interact with players during unguarded moments.

Not all the beat writers cover the teams with total seriousness all the time. Certainly Henry did not. Luis Tiant joined us as a free agent from the Red Sox in 1979. Henry heard that Tiant had a rare talent. In addition to his ability to turn pirouettes before every pitch he threw, his back facing the plate and eyes skyward, Tiant could take a shower while smoking a cigar and never get it wet.

"I asked for a demonstration," Henry said. "Tiant was known throughout baseball as one of its great free spirits and light hearts. He completely got that I was going to write a funny article and, yes, he showed me how he did it. I stood at the edge of the shower taking notes." How did he do it? "Keep moving the cigar from hand to hand," Henry says. "Lots of switching hands and moving around under the shower." With showers long having become smoke free, we will not see the likes of this special talent again.

One activity Henry shared with the players was a long-running poker game, and he was the only writer in the game. The game was most frequently high-low. I guess this was the perfect game for some of our teams, because we went through a lot of highs and a lot of lows. "The regulars that I remember were Ken Holtzman, Rivers, Munson, broadcaster Frank Messer, and usually me," Henry recalls. "I can't for the life of me remember the rest. Holtzman and Rivers were almost partners. If one of them folded, he would give the other advice on his hand." It was pretty funny to see this jive-talking black guy who murdered the English language partnering up with this Jewish guy who had a degree in business administration from the University of Illinois. I don't think it helped either of them win much, however.

"One night, the team wasn't playing well, and we were in somebody's hotel room and the phone rang, and they had Dell Alston answer it," Henry says. Dell was about the sixth outfielder on a team that needed five. He was "on the bubble," to use the current jargon. "Naturally, it was Billy, screaming for us to stop playing." It seems like baseball law that the guy with the most insecure place on the team always gets caught. Nowadays, a writer in card games with players would be rare.

Writers don't ride the team buses anymore, either. Although usually the trips were just back and forth from airports to stadiums, they provided valuable glimpses into that elusive element called "chemistry." It was on the bus that Yogi Berra slapped the harmonica out of Phil Linz's hands in 1964, which either cost Yogi's job or saved it, depending on who is spinning the tale.

Likewise, Henry was on the bus for a classic confrontation. "The Yankees got on each other all the time, especially Piniella and Hunter. They were back and forth all the time, getting on each other," Henry says. "Some of it was very funny, classic, locker-room insult humor. Then one day Mickey Rivers and Reggie Jackson were needling each other. Rivers said, 'Reginald Manuel Jackson. You got a white man's first name, a Spanish man's middle name, and a black man's last name. You don't know who you are.'

"So there's a truck passing the bus, and Reggie says to Mickey, 'That's you in 10 years, driving a truck.' And Mickey shoots back, 'Yeah, but I'll be a happy truck driver,'" Henry says. Mickey had a way of putting things that was pretty right on, and seldom did anyone nail Reggie's capacity for inner agitation. "What makes it even stranger," Henry notes, "is that Mickey got it wrong. Reggie's middle name is Martinez. Of course, you know whose middle name is Manuel. Billy Martin. Interesting transposition."

Now, with no writers on the bus, nobody ever hears that kind of stuff outside of the team and the driver. As a result, fans don't have as good an idea of what the players are really like. They become more distant, less personal, a result of being available only through far more limited pregame access and postgame interviews.

The circumstance of Henry's top billing began when he joined the team after the All-Star break in 1978. We were riddled by injuries and 14 games behind the Red Sox, the low point of the season. Typical of that year, any seemingly small event such as a hitter failing to lay down a bunt became big news throughout the city.

"This was right after the break," Henry remembers. "I had just picked up the team, and it was a Monday night against the Royals in extra innings. Billy gave Reggie the bunt sign. Now you've got to understand, Billy was turning Reggie into a DH against righties and really trying to drive him out of town. So he gives Reggie the bunt sign, and Reggie doesn't lay it down; I don't know if he tried or not, but anyway, he wasn't a good bunter even if he was trying. So Billy takes off the bunt sign, and Reggie bunted against orders. It was like he reached his breaking point. So Billy suspended Reggie for five games for bunting against orders."

Wait, there's more. "That was the same game Sparky Lyle refused to pitch another inning," Henry continues. "He'd lost the closer's job to Gossage, and I think he came in to pitch the fifth inning. Billy wanted him to pitch the sixth, but Sparky was in the clubhouse, so when Billy sent Art Fowler in to get him, Sparky told Fowler, 'Tell him I'm a short reliever, not a long reliever.' So the same game Reggie got suspended for defying the manager, Lyle defied the manager and got away with it. Billy was always looking for allies, and he thought Sparky was one, so that was why he didn't do anything.

"I didn't know about it, but Murray Chass of the *Times* had it as a note the next day, and I thought, *Wait a minute, one guy defies the manager and gets suspended, and the other guy defies the manager and gets away with it?*" Henry says. "So I spent the next few days nailing down the facts and wrote a big story in Friday's paper that there's a double standard on the Yankees because one guy, etc., which got the Yankees crazy.

"Meanwhile, the team is winning every game. Two in Minnesota, and then they go to Chicago and win three. Reggie comes back that Sunday in Chicago because the suspension is over after the game, but he will not apologize, and that makes Billy ripshit. So on the bus to the airport he lets Reggie have it. When the bus gets to the airport, all the writers phone their offices to let their editors know what's happening. I go to the newsstand to get the Sunday *Times* for the crossword puzzle, and Murray is there. We're talking about what happened, and here comes Billy on the way to the gate.

"Murray and I look at each other and start walking with Billy. That's when he said the born-and-convicted-liar line. He called Steinbrenner a liar because the boss had been convicted of a felony for making an illegal campaign contribution to Richard Nixon. Billy also had been upset because Reggie said he never talked to him, so his defense was: 'He asked me in spring training if he could drive his Royals Royce to Fort Myers, and I let him.' Yes, Billy said, 'Royals Royce.' Then he said, 'They deserve each other. One's a born liar and the other's convicted.' The kicker is that Billy stole the line from Dick Tidrow, who said it the year before about George and Billy!

"We both print the quote, Billy resigns under pressure, and there's that weird thing at the Yankee Old Timer's Game," Henry says. "They announce that Billy's coming back as manager next year. He runs out of the dugout waving his hat to a huge ovation."

Thus the stage was set for Henry's top billing a few days later. Billy was very popular with a lot of the fans, and it seemed he was most popular with the most vocal and demonstrative. To them, it looked as if Henry and Reggie had gotten Billy Martin fired. This was back in the days when it was common for bed-sheets to be hung over the upper deck with various expressions of support, opinions, and so forth. It was a way for the fans to express themselves.

"I never saw the sheet from the press box," Henry recalls. "An Associated Press photographer took a photo and gave me a copy." It still hangs in a prominent place in his living room. After all, it is not often that a mere beat writer gets top billing over a future Hall of Famer.

Here is what was written on the sheet, the second line beneath the first: "Henry Hecht sucks. Reggie, too."

An Unusual Standing Ovation

My last year in the majors was 1979. At midseason I was hitting below the Mendoza Line, and the team was stuck around .500 after winning it all the previous year. So George Steinbrenner made one of his many musical-managers moves and brought back Billy Martin, who, as I and everyone else quickly discovered, wasn't going to give me much of a chance to raise that batting average. I rode the pine and didn't like it. Who does? But it turns out the fans didn't like it, either.

One night with more than 50,000 fans in Yankee Stadium for the Red Sox, Tommy John was battling rookie Joel Finch 1–1 through four innings. But Finch yielded a homer to Jim Spencer in the fifth, and, when he booted Piniella's grounder after a Reggie homer, he was replaced by Bill "Soup" Campbell. Soup held the score to 3–2 until the seventh, when Spencer led off with a walk. Billy called me to pinch-run.

I was amazed at the reception from the crowd. Not only did they cheer, but they continued to cheer. The stood and cheered. I got a standing ovation for pinch-running!

To me, it meant that the fans knew I ought to be playing more. Howard Cosell was in the broadcast booth. Nobody, of course, knew how to lay it on like Howard. This was unprecedented! This was amazing! This was a message to Martin! Above all, it was the grateful Yankees fans' recognition of what I had contributed over the years, according to Howard.

Okay, whatever. It felt pretty good to me. It got me feeling good about myself and how it was my turn to shine and help win the game. The next batter, Bucky Dent, singled to right. *I was put in to run, right? That's what I'll do, I think.* I rounded second and downshifted at the bag, going for third.

I had gone only a little way when I noticed something. The third baseman seemed quite eager. Then I remembered. Bucky Dent hit the ball. That meant the right fielder would be playing shallow, because Bucky was about as likely to hit it over the right fielder's head as Joel Finch was to win the Cy Young Award.

And the right fielder who was playing shallow? Dwight Evans. Yes, that Dwight Evans. The Dwight Evans who had only the best arm of any right fielder I ever played with or against. In my gracious recognition of this Roy White Appreciation Night I had a bit of a brain freeze. No wonder the third baseman was eager.

I was out from the Bronx to Canarsie, which, in case you are not from New York, that's another way of saying *considerably.* Let's just say I slid to make it look closer.

I had used my quota of standing ovations for the night. The fans' reaction to my latest play was a bit less enthusiastic, though we still managed to score four runs that inning to put the game away. Joel Finch never did get a win.

Even more improbable, as I was later informed, was Howard Cosell's reaction to my being thrown out at third, right after he had gone to such lengths to praise the crowd's good judgment in recognizing my years on the field. He was speechless.

appendix

Timeline, 1965–1979

1965:
Roy White makes his major-league debut on September 7, in the first game of a doubleheader against Baltimore at Yankee Stadium. He bats for Al Downing in the seventh inning and singles. In the second game he starts at second base and goes 2–5. The Orioles sweep, 4–2 and 9–5.

Mickey Mantle is moved to left field, his first year out of center since 1952, when he replaced Joe DiMaggio. Leg injuries that plagued his entire career finally catch up to him, as he posts career lows in almost all hitting categories.

The Yankees, managed by Johnny Keane in his only full year at the job, finish 77–85, in sixth place, their worst showing and first losing season since 1925.

1966-68:
Roy White becomes the regular left fielder in 1968 after some early experiments in center, right, second, and third.

Mickey Mantle returns to center field, then moves to first base for his final two years. He finishes with 536 homers and a ticket to Cooperstown.

The Yankees return Ralph Houk as manager. After two years of finishing 10th and ninth, 1968 shows a rebound to 83–79.

1969–1975:
Roy White averages 150 games per year and doesn't miss a game in 1970, 1972, or 1973. In 1970 he records career highs of 22 homers, 94 RBIs, and a .296 average.

The Yankees finish second in 1970, then hover around .500 for several years. Bill Virdon replaces Houk in 1974, and Billy Martin replaces Virdon for the final 56 games of 1975.

1976–1979:
Roy White is on base for the Bucky Dent homer that wins the division in 1978 and hits a home run versus Kansas City to win the pennant. Roy plays his last Yankees game September 27, 1979. He pinch-hits for Fred Stanley in the ninth inning, driving in the tying run with a sacrifice fly.

Mickey Rivers is acquired from the Angels on December 11, 1975, with pitcher Ed Figueroa for Bobby Bonds. From 1976 through 1978, he averages .301 and 30 stolen bases, hitting leadoff and igniting the Yankees offense to three pennants and two World Series wins.

The Yankees win their first pennant in 12 years in 1976, losing the World Series to Cincinnati. They win the Series in 1977 and 1978.

sources

Books

Allen, Mel, and Ed Fitzgerald. *You Can't Beat the Hours*. New York: Harper & Rowe, 1964.

Hoppel, Joe. *The World Series*. St. Louis: The Sporting News, 1989.

Paige, Leroy (Satchel). *Maybe I'll Pitch Forever*. Garden City, New York: Doubleday, 1962.

Articles

Corben, Len. "Case of the Ambidextrous Pitcher." *North Shore Outlook*, August 11, 2005, p. 30.

Joyner, Ronnie. "The $1 Million Common of Chuck Goggin." *Sports Collectors Digest*, October 26, 2007, pgs. 36, 38; December 7, 2007, pgs. 20, 22.

Katz, Fred. "Johnny Sain's Big Job." *Sport*, October 1961, p. 49.

Websites

www.baseballhalloffame.org
www.baseballlibrary.com
www.baseball-reference.com
www.bronxleadershipacademy2.org
www.collegefootball.com
www.compton.k12.ca.usnbcbaseball.com
www.gonysata2.org/Awards/hall of fame/Monahan.html
    January, 2008
www.hertford.com
www.nimst.tripod.com
www.pao.hood.army.mil
www.retrosheet.org
www.theblackaces.com

Other Sources

Topps Baseball Cards, 1965: 76, 226, 245, 369, 598
Topps Baseball Cards, 1966: 234, 469
Topps Baseball Cards, 1969: 594
Topps Baseball Cards, 1970: 333, 373, 594, 654